INFORMATION TECHNOLOGY FOR HIGHER EDUCATION

INFORMATION TECHNOLOGY FOR HIGHER EDUCATION

Edited by

Moturi Ravi Kumar

M.Sc., M.Ed., M.C.A.

Lecturer in Mathematics & Computer Science

R.V.R. College of Education

Guntur–522 006

SONALI PUBLICATIONS

NEW DELHI-110002

Edition - 2022

ISBN 87-88836-34-6

Published by

SONALI PUBLICATIONS
4831/24, Ansari Road, Prahlad Street,
Darya Ganj, New Delhi-110002 (India)
Phone: 23279245 • Fax: 91-11-23253475

Printed at -
Navya Digital
Delhi - 110092

PREFACE

Information technologies have played a vital role in higher education for decades. Television started sending instruction to campuses and homes during the 1950s; before that, radio and film were used in a wide range of courses; and computers have populated labs in schools since the late 1960s. But only recently has interest in educational applications of information technology, which now includes the Internet and the World Wide Web, reached nearly universal proportions. In the past, discussion of educational technology was limited mainly to academic and teaching journals; now, almost every major newspaper has devoted at least a series of articles or a Sunday supplement to "Learning in Cyberspace," touting technology as a savior for education.

In a vast country such as India using information and communication technologies in distance education mode has the potential for cost-effective in-service education of teachers. As access to the Internet is mainly available to those living in metropolitan cities promotion of its use for education has become a cause of concern for it can only exacerbate the digital divide.

Some recent developments in information and communication technologies (ICT) have emerged as viable alternatives that can be effectively used in bridging the digital divide and for delivering learning resources at near zero cost to learners across an entire continent. One such technology that has recently emerged on the scene is the satellite radio services. The satellite radio system combines digital audio and digital data transmission (Direct Media Service), two of the most powerful technologies of the Information

Age, in the direct-to-home (DTH) mode. The text of the book is prepared for the need of students, teachers, academics & IT professionals.

Editor

CONTENTS

1

INTRODUCTION AND OVERVIEW

Information technologies have played a vital role in higher education for decades. Television started sending instruction to campuses and homes during the 1950s; before that, radio and film were used in a wide range of courses; and computers have populated labs in schools since the late 1960s. But only recently has interest in educational applications of information technology, which now includes the Internet and the World Wide Web, reached nearly universal proportions. In the past, discussion of educational technology was limited mainly to academic and teaching journals; now, almost every major newspaper has devoted at least a series of articles or a Sunday supplement to "Learning in Cyberspace," touting technology as a savior for education.

As veterans in the battle to move computers into classrooms, we in the Institute on Education and Training at RAND are naturally excited by this surge of interest. But we are also anxious, because this is not the first time technology has been touted as a savior for education, and all previous technology "revolutions" have failed, in part because they were not, technically, great improvements on prior educational tools. Of course, past failures have not been complete flops; after all, the use of instructional TV and computer-based integrated learning systems, for example, persists in schools and campuses, although mainly on the margin. And newer technologies, from CD-ROM-based multimedia products to Internet chat rooms, are potentially much more powerful than previous technologies; so they should avoid many prior technical limitations. However, like the previous technology revolutions, the impending information technology revolution also may fall far short of expectations.

With the hope that we can help the revolution move forward, we offer here a critical, constructive review of the potential opportunities that new information technologies afford higher education.

Vision of New Technology

We admit, at the outset, that we believe that information technologies can help higher education reach many of its goals. We will go even further to say that our vision is organized around the pervasive use of interactive and high-bandwidth communication networks. In particular, the model we champion is the Internet, the World Wide Web (WWW), and its generic tools (e.g., browsers such as Netscape),which are used to create and run applications (now often called "homepages"). But it is not the early Web (as late as 1995), with its static book pages rendered electronically, that we think could revolutionize education and learning. It is, instead, the emerging global information infrastructure (GII) of dynamic Web objects that will succeed the current Internet and WWW — a computational environment populated by many multimedia and interactive applications, as well as human and computer agents — which will be the focus of our discussions.

Higher-education institutions, in general, are very well represented on the Internet. This is hardly surprising: For its first 25 years, the Internet (until 1990 called the ARPANET) was inhabited mainly by universities, nonprofits, and government agencies. True, some colleges and smaller universities still lag behind, but the larger schools remain among the most extensive and most sophisticated users of Internet and Web resources — even today, as commercial sites rapidly take over cyberspace. Put most positively, the Internet is probably the only information-technology arena in which higher education has more than kept pace with the business world, both in its raw capacity and its skill in creating useful products. (On a given day, the average university classroom surely logs more Web-site "hits" than phone calls.)

Of course, many technologies other than the Internet can and do play important roles in education. Stand-alone computers run many kinds of useful instructional programs; they will continue to be important as machines drop in price even as they increase in power. And, today certainly, more educational information is delivered on CD-ROM than through networks such as the Internet. Still, we favor the Internet as a unique foundation for education because it will *eventually* include all the functionality's of the other available tools, and more. Rooted in relatively primitive network applications that transfer files of text (e.g., ftp), over the past few years, the World Wide Web has added layer upon layer of new communication protocols and document types. Now you can find Web sites that imitate almost all other communication devices and genres — audio or video, two-way or one-way, broadcast or point-to-point. But are these imitations? Perhaps it is better to view the Internet simply as a flexible new medium that can merge or encompass all old (and new) information technologies. While the Internet can mimic more traditional information media and genres, it also offers novel functionality's not found elsewhere — multi-user video games (such as "Quake"; www.idsoftware.com/), interactive soap operas (such as "The Spot"; www.thespot.com/),and online "chat" rooms (such as "V-Chat"; www.microsoft.com/ie/chat/), for instance.

Function	*Web Site Example*
Radio	*NPR*'s site (www.npr.org/) includes many of their programs, current and past, including newscasts updated every hour. *Net Radio* (www.netradio.net/) permits listeners to select different types of music, as well as "talk radio" features, at a click of the mouse. Both NPR and Net Radio use *Real Audio* (www.realaudio.com/) as a helper application.

(Contd.)

Function	*Web Site Example*
Telephone	VocalTec's *Internet Phone* (www.vocaltec.com/) provides telephone-quality, point-to-point, voice communication over the Internet. Internet Phone incurs no long-distance charges, much to the consternation of traditional long-distance providers.
Television	Many Web sites are already devoted to commercial TV; most are simply advertising, but several include substantial video. *PBS*'s "Life on the Internet" (http://www.pbs.org/internet/) was a 13-part video series made available on the Internet. It used *VDOLive*'s (www.vdolive.com/) Internet video technology and servers. *HyperTV* (www.hypertv.com/) promises to interweave traditional TV transmission and Internet browsing. MSN (www.msn.com/) acts more like a TV network than a single TV channel or program.
Newspaper	Hundreds of newspapers are now online. Some are faithful to their hardcopy versions; others are better designed for the Web. In this regard, *The New York Times on the Web* (http://www.nytimes.com/) falls about in the middle.
Phone book	*BigBook* (www.bigbook.com/) not only boasts a very complete interactive Yellow Pages for the whole nation, but also will display a map showing the location of a business, as well as reviews offered by other users.
Billboard	*CyberBillboard* (village.jos.com/-cyber/cbbdesgn.htm) will design and post digital billboards on the Web for customers.
Fax	There are any number of ways to send a fax on the Internet. Try just printing, say, a Word document to a fax "printer."

Function	*Web Site Example*
CD-ROM-based video game	As the Internet's multimedia capacity has expanded, *Nintendo* (www.nintendo.com/), *Sega* (www.sega.com/), and other video game companies that used to distribute products either on CD-ROMs or cartridges have made many new and old titles available on the Web.
Intelligent tutoring systems	*Rebel!* is an interactive, exploratory environment for learning history through simulation. It was originally configured as a standalone application, running on a macintosh; but it was reconfigured to display to, and interact with, users on any machine connected to the Web.

Figure 1.1 — The Internet and World Wide Web as Communication Channels

Supported by emerging standards such as the Common Object Request Broker Architecture (CORBA), new document formats (now called distributed objects) and communication protocols will evolve into an ever-expanding collection. These will give rise to more and more genres unique to digital networks — products that imitate no previous forms of communication. If interaction is omitted, the Internet can become instructional TV; if text and other symbolic media are omitted, it can mimic two-way video; if multi-casting is omitted, the Internet might look like a one on-one intelligent tutoring system; the Internet can even impersonate fax, radio, and newspapers. The ability of the emerging Internet to encompass just about all other information technologies is potentially critical to realizing its value for higher education.

Qualifications on the Vision

In addition to discussing how this potential could be realized in higher education, we insert a recurring theme that provides a sober counterpoint to this promising picture. We claim that information technology — or any profound innovation — leads to a fairly predictable sequence of events as it is adopted in society:

- First, it is exploited as an *enhancer*, or magnifier. The innovation is used to accomplish traditional practices (in manufacturing, services industries, even education) more efficiently or productively.
- Later, it becomes a *transformer*. It leads to new practices and products, not simply better versions of traditional ones. This shift is usually very slow and rarely smooth.

Traditional applications of new technologies can lead to improvements that are more valuable than the original version of the technology, so there is often good reason to resist fundamental change. For example, early gas-powered vehicles designed to resemble horseless carriages *are* useful. But, in the long run, the technology affords new opportunities that can be more valuable: Cars are *much more* useful. Yet this transformation is not without great uncertainty and great cost — in time, money, and fundamental restructuring.

Cars dominate carriages only if we build paved roads, provide service stations, and pass laws that govern speed and the transport of goods. This idea is not new (it parallels the economic distinction between *process* and *product innovation*, for example) but will arise often in our discussions. We discuss many possible applications of information technologies in higher education. Some relatively traditional applications are attractive in the short term because they can help cut costs. There is certainly no reason to reject them. But innovative applications could help solve other important problems in the long term, even though they may not save money in the short term. The difficulty is that some of these applications are not just technology fixes or add-ons; they will require that the higher-education community think hard about its mission, its organization, and its willingness to invest in change — even in a time of fiscal tightening.

The Plan

Our discussion begins with examples that illustrate many interesting, cutting-edge applications. But, unlike many discussions of education in cyberspace, our focus is on information technology as a tool to help solve the central problems in higher education. We consider:

- the need to reduce costs and to increase productivity in the face of dwindling resources
- the challenges of an expanding and increasingly diverse student population (including minorities and geographically isolated rural or inner-city populations, as well as lifelong learners who must retool their skills)
- the necessity of adapting to changes in industry and social demands (a broad shift away from manual laborers and toward knowledge workers)
- competition with a growing number of external providers proprietary, for-profit firms not associated with colleges or universities (often specializing in corporate training but almost always exploiting information technology).

Information technologies can affect many facets of higher education, much as they do almost every service industry. We focus here on the opportunities that appear unique to education, ignoring many important applications. For example, we pass over the different ways technologies already streamline student-record maintenance, budgeting, payroll, and general administration. There is already a large body of literature on the costs and benefits to business of computer and communication technologies, and educational applications add few new insights to this field. Rather, we look at applications of information technologies from the inner missions of higher education outward:

- the benefits for learning and instruction delivery that new information technologies can promise
- the ways in which information technologies can help provide tools for building instruction
- the tools information technologies can offer for improving decision making and community-building within higher education
- the manner in which information technologies can help connect higher-education institutions to industry and society as a whole.

In these discussions we summarize available data on how technology helps overcome important challenges to higher education. But we also include many sidebars of current or emerging "best practice." Our arguments are illustrated by anecdotes, or examples, partly because they bring abstract claims to life and partly because there are few hard data on what new technologies can really do for higher education.

We next summarize the evidence about these applications to clarify those that are less than they seem; uncover others that may be more promising, although perhaps less obviously so or less colorful; and identify the hidden costs — costs that must be paid if even the most promising uses of information technology in higher education are to deliver what they suggest. This summary leads to a more complete discussion of the barriers to realizing the potentials of new technologies in higher education and, finally, to some broad policy issues that surround the resolution of these problems.

2

INTERNET EDUCATION

Education on the Internet simply means putting information on one computer where it can be seen by others on the Internet. You might put stories, articles, poems, pictures, or music on the Internet. You can sell what you publish or give it away. Although the commercial and marketing possibilities are creating enormous interest, the bulk of what is published today on the Internet is available for free. Companies are finding that traditional advertising techniques don't transfer well to the Internet; instead they are supplying detailed information and participating in technical forums in which their products are discussed.

A Quick History of Internet Education Techniques

Education on the Internet basically consists of making computer files available on one computer, usually called a server, and allowing others to view or download them via other computers, usually called clients. Finding and looking at these files always involves several steps:

1. Find the computer site with the file(s) you want.
2. Login to that computer.
3. Find the file(s).

4. Transfer the file(s).
5. Disconnect.
6. Look at the file(s) on your own system.

Programmers and computer technical administrators have used this procedure for many years. Now Gopher, WWW, and WAIS make this process incredibly easy and much more efficient for everyone else. In fact, Gopher, WWW, and WAIS take very similar steps behind the scenes as you browse the Internet, blissfully oblivious to the details.

File Transfer Protocol (FTP)

File Transfer Protocol, or **FTP,** is the original method of using the Internet to transfer files between different computer systems. FTP is available on many systems and allows you to reach out from one computer to another and retrieve files. FTP requires that you know the name of the computer to which you wish to connect and have a login ID and password for that computer. Friends or colleagues who have the passwords to each other's accounts can use FTP. Or you can set a computer up for anonymous use.

For years **anonymous FTP** was the method of choice for educating on the Internet. Anonymous FTP (a term that's used as a noun and a verb on the Internet) does not require the client to have an ID for the publishing computer in order to connect and download files. Users login with the ID *anonymous* and usually are asked to give their e-mail address as a password. Even this is sometimes not required.

Anonymous FTP allowed true education to occur on the Internet, because once you made your information available via anonymous FTP, anyone on the Internet could download it. This method proved so popular among the programmers and technical people (most Internet users in those days) that thousands of FTP sites (computers with files available for anonymous FTP downloads) sprang up over the years. A wealth of software, text files, and other information was scattered among thousands of computers. The problem was finding the site that had what you wanted and then locating the information in the thousands of files that might be stored on that same computer.

Archie—Indexing FTP Sites

In 1990 Peter Deutsch and Alan Emtage, grad students at McGill University in Canada, came up with **Archie**, an interesting approach to solving this problem. (The name *Archie* actually derives from the word *archives*. When similar programs were created later, their authors used characters in the Archie comic books to name them. Veronica is actually an acronym for Very Easy Rodent-Oriented Net-wide Index to Computer Archives, *rodent* being a reference to the Gopher servers for Veronica indexes. Jughead, another character, is short for Jonzy's Universal Gopher Hierarchy Excavation and Display.) Deutsch and Emtage set up one computer to connect automatically to a certain number of FTP servers every night and download their directory structures and indexes. They added these indexes to a database and then would allow anyone on the Internet to connect to their machine and run a search program. The search program allowed the user to search by file name and would return all the occurrences of a particular file name, complete with date, directory path, and FTP site address. The Archie program could also e-mail the results to you. Clearly, this was a tremendous service to the Internet community and, as great ideas often do, it spread quickly.

Although Archie allowed users to quickly find the FTP sites with the most recent copies of particular files, it wasn't especially user friendly. While connected to an FTP site, you could make your way through the various directories by typing in the appropriate change directory (or cd) command, but you couldn't view a file to determine whether it contained what you were looking for.

Gopher and Gopher+

In 1991 the University of Minnesota made all this easier. In attempting to make information available campus-wide, a small team of programmers led by Mark McCahill designed the Gopher protocol. This major innovation in Internet usability embodied several simple ideas:

- A simple interface that novice users could use without training
- Minimal bandwidth requirements so the network wouldn't be overloaded

- Short connections between the client and server programs so the server could quickly handle a client's request and move on to the next
- "Stateless" connections (no memory of previous contacts) between client and server, so the server wouldn't have to remember what stage each client was at
- Access to such popular Internet services as FTP, Usenet News, and telnet

This approach resulted in a menu like system that allows users either to see the contents of a file or to follow a link to other menus or files on another system. Thus was born the ability to "browse" the Internet, because Gopher allows you to read the text files you come across and, depending on your computer, to view pictures or hear sound embedded in the files you select. Gopher makes moving through directories and downloading programs much simpler than they are through FTP.

The success of Gopher's simple interface led to explosive growth in the number of Gopher servers in the United States and then around the world. And it led to extensions of the original Gopher protocol to allow for such things as electronic forms, abstracts, alternate data formats, or views, and the ability to store *meta-information* (or behind-the-scenes information) about the files (such as modification date, file size, language, and administrator of the file). These changes are incorporated in the Gopher+ protocol, which has increased the capabilities of the Gopher system. Unfortunately, not all Gopher client programs have been updated to work with Gopher+.

Veronica—Indexing Gopher Sites

The hundreds, then thousands, of Gopher servers springing up created the need to be able to find specific items among all the Gopher sites. Now the University of Nevada at Reno (UNR) got its chance to contribute to the quest for easy Net access. There, Steven Foster of UNR applied the Archie model to *Gopher space*, the collection of all items in all Gopher servers in the world, and called it *Veronica*. That is, he set up a computer to connect to all the registered Gopher servers and directed it to follow their menus, collecting menu and file names as it went. The compilation was searchable, and what was especially nice was that the results showed up as one or more Gopher menus, which the user could follow directly to the files or Gopher servers themselves. As the obvious utility of this system became known, universities around the world began running Veronica servers, which soon forced each to introduce its offerings with an opening screen that allows the user to select a server and type of search to use.

The dynamic nature of this database meant that you could do a Veronica search one day and find three matches and then the next day do the same search and find 10 or 12 more, depending on what had been added. Suddenly, Gopher became much more powerful—instead of working your way through menu after menu, you could connect to a Veronica server and search all the menus and files with a specific word or phrase that might appear in their titles. Searching their contents was another matter. For that you needed something like WAIS.

Wide Area Information Server (WAIS)

WAIS (pronounced *ways*), started in 1988, was an experimental project designed to come up with easier ways to search Internet files for content. The team was headed by Brewster Kahle, then of Thinking Machines Corporation (a producer of parallel-processing computers), in cooperation with Apple Computer, Dow Jones, and KPMG Peat Marwick. The goal was to create a way to easily search large amounts of text, images, or other files scattered among different computers.

Based on the ANSI standard search-and-retrieval protocol Z39.50, then under development, WAIS allows users to type in a question in their natural language—it does not force the user to learn and use a particular computer language or syntax. The WAIS protocol then does the dirty work of translating the query into a WAIS computer language query format and sends it off to various WAIS servers on the Internet. The servers in turn search their full-text indexes and return to the user a list of hits, or matches, ranked by how well they match the original query. When the user selects a hit, the WAIS server retrieves the document that matches.

The companies that had formed the development team made the details and program source code for WAIS publicly available because they realized that WAIS would be much more useful—and have a shot at becoming an industry standard—if it were commonly accepted and used by others across the Internet.

Although WAIS as a front end, or client, hasn't caught on nearly as well as Gopher or WWW, it has become the search mechanism of choice, running in the background of other front-end systems.

World-Wide Web (WWW)

The World-Wide Web was invented by Tim Berners-Lee in 1989 in an attempt to efficiently store research data at CERN, the European Particle Physics Laboratory in Geneva, Switzerland. Berners-Lee, a consultant with a background in text-processing software development, wanted a system that would make it easy for various researchers to build up separate bodies of information and then link them electronically by matching the real links in the information. He based the system on the concept of hypertext, or text with links that can be followed electronically to other documents, files, sounds, images, or even programs. The WWW system allows hypertext to link files on different computer systems. The main advantages, or power, of hypertext lie in its ability to link different pieces of information in simple ways, at exactly the spot at which you thought of the connection. In a way, hypertext links are like footnotes, except that they are easier to follow and can be of any length. For example, if this page were hypertext, it could have links to the history of hypertext, examples of hypertext, and even a video of someone discussing hypertext. This can be distracting if you want to just read from beginning to end with no detours. But the beauty of hypertext is that no one forces you to follow all the links. You follow what interests you and ignore the rest.

The World-Wide Web system is known by various names. WWW, W3, and Web are intuitive, but because it uses the Hyper-Text Transfer Protocol (HTTP) and Hyper-Text Markup Language (HTML), the servers are technically called *HTTP servers*. Although we'll refer to them as Web or *WWW servers*, you will often see *HTTP servers* used in technical documentation.

One important contribution of WWW was the *Uniform Resource Locator (URL)*. This address system allows you to declare the name and port number (a *port* is like a doorway, or loading dock, of a computer) of the host computer, the protocol (type of connection, such as FTP, Gopher, and so on), and the directory path and file name, all on one line. URLs have become a convenient method of passing a link on to some data source on the Internet. Net users made it common practice to include a URL for their *home page* (a personal spot on the Web) at the end of their e-mail messages. In fact, the URL system has been incorporated in the Gopher server software put out by the University of Minnesota.

The other main innovation of WWW was *HTML, or Hyper Text Markup Language*. Briefly (Chapter 4 goes into more depth), HTML is a relatively simple set of codes that turns ordinary text into hypertext when viewed by a WWW browser. The beauty of the system is that it need not be viewed on the same system that created it. In other words, an HTML file created on a Macintosh will look pretty much the same when viewed on a PC or a UNIX workstation. And what is more important, all the links function in exactly the same way. The ability to move a single file between different types of computer systems and have it work the same way in all of them is called *portability*, an essential ingredient when you want the whole world to use something.

Although WWW was seeing some success—the number of servers was increasing steadily—the creation of a WWW browser called Mosaic by the National Center for Supercomputing Applications (NCSA) in Champaign-Urbana, Illinois, led to an explosion of interest in WWW. This program, which was being given away free, was created first for X-Windows on UNIX and soon after for Macintosh and PCs running Microsoft Windows. Often called the killer application of the Internet, Mosaic made the Internet sexy by adding support for graphics. Gopher was nice and easy to use, but Mosaic was fun and much more impressive in what it could display, mostly because publishers could interweave text and images in documents to create the equivalent of a glossy brochure distributed on the Internet. Among the more popular early demonstrations of WWW was a tour of the Krannert Art Museum at the University of Illinois. Gopher could provide the same information but as menus, and the user could look at one element at a time but not the whole thing. That is, with Gopher you keep coming back to a menu from which you choose a text file, an image file, or a sound file. With WWW you can look at text and images together – perhaps several images side by side and surrounded by text.

This difference has a big effect on the visual effects of a document browsed on the Internet. Imagine being able to use buttons or links from the colorful WWW page that activate sound files or run movie files that start as soon as you select that button. This capability wows the user but puts a different load on the network and requires more sophisticated equipment. Gopher was designed for use by slow, relatively old computers, with no large drain on network resources. But WWW and Mosaic were designed in high-intensity computing environments, in which all participants had fast Internet connections and sophisticated workstations (although they will work on a 386 PC running Windows with a 14,400-baud modem).

When you start education on the Internet, it is good to remember that many people who want access to your information may in fact have slow Internet connections and not very powerful computers. If your company's home page takes 10 minutes to download and can only be appreciated on a top-of-the-line workstation, you may not get the audience you want. The reality of WWW is that graphic presentations are more attractive and exciting than plain text, but people won't see them if it takes five minutes or more for those images to appear on their screens. Your images won't slow down text-only Web browsers like Lynx (because Lynx simply ignores them), but those using text-mode browsers won't see and enjoy your images.

Summary

Internet education consists of posting or putting material on the Internet where it can be viewed or downloaded from other computers. This process has evolved both in the user interface and in the tools that have been built to enable people to find them.

We've covered a lot of ground in this chapter, so let's review the terms—you're going to need them to understand the rest of this book:

- **FTP** (File Transfer Protocol) is a tried-and-true method for transferring files, but users have to know which computer has the directory and file they want, and the process is confusing to the novice.
- **Archie** is a program that actively goes out and indexes all the known anonymous FTP servers and makes that information freely available via the Archie client program.
- **Gopher** presents menus that lead to files that you can view easily, as well as **links** to other servers. The links are easy for the novice to follow, but with thousands of Gopher servers all over the world, finding what you want is often a problem.
- **Veronica** does for Gopher servers what Archie did for FTP sites. It goes out and indexes all the known Gopher servers and provides a simple method for searching that index. The results then appear as more Gopher menus.
- **WAIS** creates indexes of the full text of files, which it then allows you to search by writing a simple query in natural language. It then applies that query to a collection of full-text indexes, supplying you with a list of those documents that most closely match. You can narrow your search by repeating the process. For example, a search on *wine* might list hundreds of documents that you can then narrow down to those wines from California or Chile or France.
- **WWW** presents hypertext, with links and images embedded in the text. This creates a powerful visual effect. Unfortunately, it does not lend itself to Veronica or Archie searches, although new indexing methods are being developed with a great deal of success. It is usually best to use a computer with fast Internet connections to browse WWW servers.

Three of the most popular publishing protocols are Gopher, World-Wide Web (WWW), and Wide Area Information Server (WAIS). They are three different protocols, or techniques for doing basically the same thing—locating a computer that has something you want, connecting to it, finding the file you're interested in, and then downloading or viewing it. Each consists of computers that act as servers, which wait for requests from other computers (**clients**), and then send the files you request back over the Internet. **Internet** publishers build servers. Internet browsers and surfers use clients.

3

Internet Browsing

You need not go through all these steps now, and they are not meant to scare you off or make the process seem intimidating. Instead, they are meant as a guideline or sort of check list for you to use to keep track of all the various elements involved.

Joining the Internet Community

Think of the Internet as a place to which you are moving and that you want to fit into. It is a community with its own set of traditions and values. And as in any community (in this case a tremendously large community), smaller groups gather to discuss different issues. Your first job is to join the Internet community in the sense of learning how to make your way around and how to fit in. On the Internet you'll find a community of individuals, companies, and organizations that are discussing issues, modifying software, and creating new tools and techniques for education on the Internet, as well as publishing the most amazing variety of information. Keeping abreast of their activities through Usenet newsgroups and e-mail mailing lists and tracking the relevant subjects through Gopher and WWW indexes are essential parts of your education process because, like it or not, you are joining a community, and you need to be aware of what's going on out there.

The first step is to start getting to know the people, organizations, and issues that shape what you do on the Internet. You can simply watch and read without posting messages, if you want. *Lurking,* the Net term for *eavesdropping,* is an accepted and common practice on the Internet. When you feel more comfortable, you can start to offer your experiences, opinions, and questions.

Usenet Newsgroups

Usenet News is an extremely large, international, cooperatively run system for exchanging messages. Usenet News is not the same as newspaper news, although there's a company called Clarinet that provides Associated Press and Reuters newsfeeds through Usenet News for a fee. Most of Usenet News consists of messages from individuals, which are like e-mail, except that they are divided by topics. Usenet News is organized into thousands of hierarchically arranged newsgroups, each of which focuses on a specific subject. Anyone can send and receive these messages. Depending on your site, you may get a full newsfeed or only partial information—certain newsgroups might not be carried. Disk space often is the limiting factor because a full Usenet newsfeed, consisting of all messages from all newsgroups all over the Internet, generates more than 5,400 megabytes per month.

A newsgroup is basically a subject area that is created so that those who are interested in that subject may exchange messages. They are hierarchically arranged, starting from some major categories:

- *comp*—computer science and computer-related topics.
- *news*—Usenet News network information. Check out news, newusers, questions and news, announce new users.
- *rec*—recreational or hobby activities.
- *sci*—hard sciences (except computer science).
- *soc*—social issues.
- *alt*—alternative newsgroups, which vary widely in subject matter and are less concerned with rules.
- *clari*—the commercial news service called Clarinet.

Other categories are often specific to a country or a university. And by no means are all newsgroups in English. New newsgroups are created by vote, except in the alt newsgroups, where the process is less formal.

News-reading programs exist for almost any computer platform conceivable—from mainframes to plain vanilla DOS PCs. Usually, the first step is to verify that you have access to a newsfeed. Then download or buy news-reading software and point it at the Usenet News server you'll be using. You'll soon see a long list of newsgroups. (I saw more than 8,000 newsgroups when I did this last at the University of California at Los Angeles, but UCLA has a Clarinet feed, which adds several thousand newsgroups.) You then select those newsgroups to which you wish to "subscribe." (There's no charge unless you license a commercial service such as Clarinet.) This isn't a permanent decision—it just helps narrow the focus a little.

Once you've subscribed to some newsgroups, you'll see (depending on your news reader) a number of "threads" or discussion chains. Reading the messages is very much like reading e-mail. An excellent starting point is Usenet Info Center, run by Kevin Atkinson, a 17-year-old student from Maryland.

Usenet newsgroups are an extremely dynamic source of information on the Internet. The messages look like e-mail but won't pile up in your mailbox. People pick the newsgroups that interest them and periodically monitor their threads (discussions) to see what is happening. Asking questions is fine after you've monitored the group for a little while and looked at any *FAQ* (Frequently Asked Questions) files available.

Alternative newsgroups are the easiest to create, and they are often formed as an immediate reaction to something, either a new piece of software or a new protocol or just an idea. Later, if a subject gains wider interest, it might be voted in as an official newsgroup in comp or one of the other domains. The new newsgroup might even split off into subgroups, focusing on specific aspects of a subject. This usually happens because the experts don't want to be bothered by lots of beginner questions.

Here are some newsgroups to check out. More are listed in each chapter's resource table:

- *comp.infosystems* discusses various types of information servers, past, present, and future.
- *comp.infosystems.announce* lists new information servers. It's one place that new WWW, Gopher, and WAIS sites are announced.
- *alt.answers* is where many newsgroups post their FAQ's and other documentation files. Monitoring alt.answers is a good way to keep track of at least some ways in which the Internet is growing.

FAQ (Frequently Asked Questions) Files

FAQ files are often extremely useful repositories of beginner and intermediate questions in different areas. They are usually composed by the regular readers of a newsgroup, so that habitués aren't constantly distracted by questions from newcomers. By making all the usual questions and answers available, the newsgroup can concentrate on newer, more interesting issues.

FAQs pop up on the most amazing subjects, and they are periodically reposted to the Usenet newsgroup alt.answers.

RFCs

RFCs (Requests for Comment) are a valuable resource for the more technically inclined; I mention them here because they demonstrate an important part of Internet culture: the development of new technology through open and widespread discussion. The RFC process works as follows. First, someone develops an idea (which could be a new protocol, standard, or even a new type of service or specific tool); when they start to get serious about it, they write up an RFC document, which describes the idea in detail. At that point people start using the material and suggest changes, improvements, and alternatives. This discussion can result in amendments to the original RFCs or new RFCs of their own. The titles may sound computer nerdish, but there's nothing like source documents. And that's what RFCs are.

Eventually, either the idea dies because of lack of interest, or it becomes a recognized guidepost (*standard* has a more official meaning) for Internet programmers, developers, and users. In this way the Internet grows in sophistication by encouraging the open development and sharing of ideas.

Mailing Lists

Mailing lists are e-mail-based systems for carrying on discussion groups. (*Note:* You'll hear these referred to as list servers or listservs as well, but list servers are actually the hardware/software for mailing list administration.) Basically, a computer is set up to accept mail at a certain address and redirect it to all members of the list. The list members do not even need to know each other, so long as they have "subscribed" to the list. Although many mailing lists are mirrored, or duplicated on Usenet newsgroups, many are available only as mailing lists. One advantage of mailing lists is that you will get the messages whether you look for them or not, usually within a few hours of when they are sent. So if you're the type who needs reminding, you'll like them. Mailing lists are also easy to create and so are useful for timely or focused topics with a limited audience. One-way mailing lists are often used for announcements of product upgrades.

Additionally, most mailing lists have archives, in which all their correspondence is saved. You should learn how to search these archives; they are an excellent resource. When you join a mailing list, you usually will receive a message that describes all the commands available for that list. If the list offers search features, they'll be mentioned there. If it doesn't, or if you don't want to subscribe to the list, try searching some Internet indexers to see if someone has put together an archive for that particular mailing list. I've found several this way. Mailing list archives can be a useful source of information and a record of discussions of issues of interest. Knowing how to retrieve all messages containing specific key words can be quite helpful. The following are some mailing lists that focus on Internet issues:

- *announce@is.internic.net*—This announcements-only mailing list is for anyone interested in getting current information about InterNIC and the services it provides. Send e-mail to listserv@is.internic.net, and in the body of the message type Subscribe announce [your name].

- *nics@is.internic.net*—This moderated list (each message is approved or controlled by the moderator) is intended for staff at midlevel, campus, and discipline-specific network information centers (NICs). Content includes InterNIC services aimed specifically at NICs, and mail sent to this list will be oriented to providing services, including new training resources and documentation, to end users. Send e-mail to listserv@is.internic.net in the body of the message type Subscribe nics [your name].
- *net-resources@is.internic.net*—This announcements-only list is a group effort of people all over the Internet to concentrate announcements of new resources on one list. It contains only announcements of new tools and resources available over the Internet. If you would like more information about participating in the Net resources list by becoming a monitor, send a note to scout@internic.net.
- RFC announcements are distributed via two mailing lists: the IETF-Announce list (IETF stands for Internet Engineering Task Force), and the RFC-DIST list. You don't want to be on both lists.

Magazines and Journals (Print)

Newsstand and postal subscription magazines and journals that focus entirely on the Internet are starting to arrive on the scene, and established magazines are paying more attention to the Internet and the subject of cyberspace. Even *Newsweek* has a regular section called Cyber-scope, which often includes URLs for interesting sites. Here are some examples of print magazines, available by subscription or at the newsstand, about the Internet:

Internet Business Advantage

$99/year (12 issues). This magazine is published by Wentworth Worldwide Media.

Internet Business Journal

$149/year (12 issues). This journal offers Internet business advice and includes a column called Internet Advertising Review. It is published by Michael Strangelove, author of *How to Advertise on the Internet.*

Internet World

$29/year (12 issues). This magazine is put out by MecklerMedia and offers interviews, columns, and advice for both new and experienced Internet users.

NetGuide

$23/year (12 issues). This magazine, published by CMP Publishing, Inc., bills itself as the "Guide to Online Services and the Internet."

Wired

$40/year (12 issues). This magazine has good interviews and prides itself on reporting on the latest and boldest in computer technology. It is available at newsstands.

Online Magazines and Journals

Online magazines are growing rapidly. In the list that follows I've included both print magazines that are starting to offer some or all of their text online, as well as true online magazines and journals that are published entirely on the Internet. You should check them out for both content and style. Some are specifically oriented to Internet publishing issues, whereas others are computer magazines that talk about Internet issues, among other things. As with any online service you come across, elements of their layout style and design may be worth emulating. Hundreds of other online journals and "zines" focus on non-computer topics. Following are just a few of the magazines and journals available online.

Computer-Mediated Communications Magazine

CMC Magazine is a free, entirely online publication that does not accept advertising. It is edited by John December, co-author of *World Wide Web Unleashed,* and reports on people, events, technology, public policy, culture, practices, research, and applications of computer-mediated communication. *Computer-mediated communication* is the academic term for what goes on when people communicate with each other via computer. WWW, Gopher, and Internet servers are a subset of computer-mediated communication.

E-mail, Usenet News, and mailing lists are other examples of computer-mediated communication. *CMC Magazine* also publishes opinions and essays about issues related to computer-mediated communication.

GNN (Global Network Navigator)

This WWW site developed by O'Reilly and Associates is one of the best and most popular examples of Internet education. It combines an online journal with links to Internet services and the O'Reilly book catalog.

HotWired

This is the online version of *Wired* magazine, and it is considerably different from the print version. *HotWired* has five channels that the editors call "doorways into the digital revolution." These include technology, "way new" journalism, the arts, commerce, and electronic conversation. Unfortunately, using them requires registration, which is free so far.

Public-Access Computer Systems Review

This free journal published by the University of Houston is primarily aimed at librarians and others who maintain publicly accessible computers.

San Jose Mercury News

This daily newspaper in California's Silicon Valley has tons of computer industry and Internet news and is available by online subscription.

St. Petersburg Times Interactive Media

This is an experimental site for the Interactive Media Department of the *St. Petersburg Times* in Florida.

TechWeb

This site by CMP Publications, Inc., offers links to many of the CMP magazines, including *Communications Week, Comm Week International, Computer Reseller News, Computer Retail Week, Electronic Buyers News, Electronic Engineering Times,*

Home PC, Information Week, Interactive Age, Internet Business Report, Netguide, Network Computing, OEM Magazine, Open Systems Today, VAR Business, and *Windows Magazine*. As of May 1995 access to the last three months of its articles was free and entirely searchable.

Ziff-Davis Publishing

This site offers links to many of the Ziff-Davis magazines, including *PC Magazine, PCWeek, PC/Computing, MacWeek, MacUser, Computer Shopper,* and *Windows Sources*. Unfortunately, it does not provide full text, but only a sampling of what's in the print version.

Internet Sites and Services of Interest to Internet Education

Look around the Internet for relevant standards and operating procedures. Sometimes these will come out in FAQ files or in comments on mailing lists or in newsgroups. Again, the point here is to know what the boundaries are, whether they are legal, institutional, or just "good taste." The point is to be a good Internet citizen. To do that you need to know the rules, written as well as unwritten.

The following sites offer Internet guidelines and reference information that you might find useful:

InterNIC

This site offers detailed information on the operation and resources of the Internet itself. The InterNIC is really three different services, maintained by separate companies under contract with the National Science Foundation. The service areas are Information Services (run by General Atomics), Directory and Database Services (run by AT&T), and Registration Services by Network Solutions, Inc.

Quality, Guidelines, and Standards for Internet Information Resources

This is a collaborative gathering of thoughts and ideas on the subject of improving information servers of all kinds.

The Directory of Electronic Journals, Newsletters, and Academic Discussion Lists

The Association of Research Libraries helps to maintain this site, which gathers links to online publications.

Organizations and Associations

You may not be a joiner, but you should be aware of these organizations, because they will be helping to shape the Internet in the years to come:

The Internet Society

This international nonprofit society's principal purpose is to "maintain and extend the development and availability of the Internet and its associated technologies and applications—both as an end in itself, and as a means of enabling organizations, professions, and individuals worldwide to more effectively collaborate, cooperate, and innovate in their respective fields and interests."

The Electronic Frontier Foundation (EFF)

The EFF is a nonprofit civil liberties organization working to protect freedom of expression, privacy, and access to online resources and information. It was founded in July 1990 by John Barlow, Mitch Kapor (founder of Lotus), Steve Wozniak (cofounder of Apple), and others to ensure that the principles embodied in the U.S. Constitution and the U.S. Bill of Rights are protected as new communications technologies emerge.

Internet Engineering Task Force (IETF)

The IETF is a large open international community of network designers, operators, vendors, and researchers concerned with the evolution of Internet architecture and the smooth operation of the Internet. It is open to any interested individual.

The World-Wide Web Consortium (W3C)

W3C operates under the leadership of Tim Berners-Lee, the author of WWW, and was formed to document and encourage the development of a common set of tools and basic programs for continued WWW development.

Electronic Privacy Information Center (EPIC)

EPIC, based in Washington, D.C., is a public interest organization established in 1994 to focus public attention on emerging privacy issues relating to the National Information Infrastructure (better known as the Information Superhighway), such as the Clipper Chip, the Digital Telephony proposal, medical records privacy, national identification systems, and the sale of consumer data. EPIC is sponsored by the Fund for Constitutional Government and Computer Professionals for Social Responsibility.

Internet Indexers and Directories

Many excellent books and online guides are available if you need help finding what's out there. Indexes, catalogs, and resource directories abound on the Internet; some that you may find useful.

Make notes as you search through this material, because later you will want to be sure that your service is listed in these indexes, directories, newsgroups, and mailing lists. Plus, the problems you have now will be similar to the challenges facing your potential users. Keep notes and learn from this experience. You'll never be less familiar with the Internet than you are today.

Also, learn from your competitors. Pay attention to how servers are set up and how documents are arranged, as well as what special features they provide to their users. For example, many sites allow you to search by key term, but one equipment manufacturer allows you to search by picture. You start with general categories and narrow down to the specific part. The company also has built and patented its own searching system.

Pay attention to feedback, searching, and charging mechanisms to see how easy and intuitive they are to use and which charging systems they are using.

Netiquette

Netiquette, short for network etiquette, is important. It is far easier to offend someone or tread on someone's toes when you can't see their face. Likewise, it is far easier to take offense because online interaction excludes nuances of rhythm, mood, and context and all body language. Here are some rules to live by:

1. Never respond rashly to provocation on the Internet. Although "flame wars" (angry messages are called *flames*) have often broken out on un-moderated mailing lists and Usenet newsgroups, no one encourages the practice. If you must respond, do it offline (that is, in private e-mail, not to the group).
2. Criticize ideas, not people. Try to be as constructive in your criticism as possible.
3. Watch or lurk for a while in any mailing list or newsgroup to get a feel for the tone and to avoid asking "newbie" (newcomer) questions.
4. Do your homework before asking questions in a mailing list or newsgroup. Look for the relevant FAQ files and archives to avoid asking questions that have already been answered millions of times.
5. Think carefully before sending a message. Remember that you are making your reputation internationally through the messages you send out. And messages last far longer than you'd expect.
6. When you ask for responses and say you'll summarize for the list, do it.
7. Answer questions when you can, but check whether others have already supplied the information.
8. Stay on the topic of the newsgroup or mailing list. No matter how strongly you feel about a subject, it is not appropriate to send information or opinions about it to unrelated groups.

Identifying Your Competition

A word about competition might be appropriate here. Remember that the Internet was built, and continues to expand, on the basis of cooperation. You should think about this if you find other services offer similar information or competing products on the Internet. Perhaps you can offer to link to their service if they'll link to yours. Or you might want to join forces with your competitor to form a more comprehensive subject-oriented server. Remember that this is a new medium and the old rules don't always apply.

Competition may not be quite the right word in your case, depending on the nature of the server and service you want to establish. But it is important to be aware of what similar servers already are doing on the Internet. Ideally, your server can work in combination with others to provide broader, more detailed resources to the Internet community instead of striving to kill someone off. Remember, the Internet has reached today's interesting state only because of the incredible spirit of cooperation that it has somehow inspired.

Defining Your Goals

What can you sensibly hope to attain by educating on the Internet? Why do you want to publish on the Internet? Do you really know what you hope to gain? Here are a few services that you might be able to offer:

- Special information not available elsewhere
- Collation and organization of information and links to information in a specific subject area
- Advertising for your business or organization
- Advertising of your own expertise

Or you might want to publish on the Internet because doing so decreases the amount of time your staff spends searching for or providing information, because you want to experiment with new technology that may benefit you or your company, or because you want to sell things and make money.

One advantage of defining your goals early is that it enables you to look at how others are achieving similar goals. You can become more analytical as you scour the Internet, noting the techniques each site uses and adding them to your repertoire.

And I should say something about experimenting and keeping your goals loosely defined. The Internet is in its infancy as a method of communication, and all the implications are not yet clear. More than one company has found that a side benefit of education on the Internet became more important and potentially more profitable than its original goal. AMP, Inc., a builder of electrical connectors, started with the idea of putting its catalog of 80,000 parts on CD-ROMs.

Then its customers (mostly high-tech companies) urged AMP to go to the Internet. In the process the company developed a unique scheme for finding exactly the right part by picture, name, or part number. Among other things, AMP found that its sales personnel started selling a wider range of parts than before. AMP has patented the interface it developed and is starting to sell it. You never can tell what you're going to learn and how useful it will be for others.

Identifying Your Audience

What do you know about your audience? If you want to publish information about Macintosh computers, you'll be able to store files in Macintosh formats and ignore other file formats. On the other hand, if you want all those interested in political science to read your work—no matter whether they're coming from a Macintosh, Sun Microsystems workstation, PC, or mainframe—you should plan to put all your documents in a portable format such as plain text or HTML or in a variety of formats.

Who is going to be happy to see your information on the Internet? Or whom do you want to come to your site? The time you spend thinking about your audience will pay off. If the members of your audience tend to flock to certain newsgroups or e-mail lists, you'll want to be sure to announce your server in those places. And you might want to consider offering to archive those newsgroups or mailing lists as a service (and good advertising). If someone is already doing this, you might consider offering to mirror, or duplicate, their service as a way to decrease the load on their server or staff. Here are some questions to ask yourself, broken into categories:

Location

- Is your potential audience limited to a certain geographical area?
- Will there be any overseas interest in your site?
- Is your audience limited to certain identifiable subnets? For example, if you want to sell a service to an institution with a clearly defined range of Internet Protocol (IP) addresses, you could rely on the IP screening capabilities in almost all Gopher, WWW, and WAIS servers. However, if your users will be

scattered all over the Internet, you might have to use individual password-based authentication instead, which is technologically more difficult and requires much more administrative overhead. (For an explanation of subnets see IP Addresses, Subnets, and Domains, a sidebar later in this chapter.)

- Is this site going to be internal, reserved only for your company or organization?

Equipment

- Do you have any reason to expect that your audience will use a certain type of computer?
- Does your audience have hardware or software limitations that would affect how you design your server?
- Do you expect that your audience will primarily be dialing in from home, or will your clients have direct (cable) connections to the Internet? For dial-ins you'll want to make sure that downloading information over a slow modem does not take forever (more than a minute or two), and if it does, perhaps you should rethink the information you want to display. Don't make your files any bigger than you have to.

Characteristics

- Is there anything that members of your audience have in common?
- Which foreign language(s) will be necessary?
- Do all your potential clients follow a certain newsgroup or e-mail list?
- Do they all use similar computers or software?

Security and Access

- Is your site open to anyone, or will you be limiting access?
- Do any IP subnets clearly define your groups? Providing or limiting access to all or part of your server is possible with most server software. You often can designate different access restrictions for different directories of your server.

What If I Don't Know?

If you don't know what kind of audience to expect, you should consider adding a poll to your server. That way you can learn more about the people who connect to your server and decide later whether to focus more narrowly or broadly. Depending on the audience, you might post some questions to a newsgroup or mailing list. Or you might persuade someone already running a server to let you post your questions. The responses could be e-mailed to you. Don't forget the possibility of contacting other, more experienced Web, Gopher, or WAIS providers to find out what they think you might expect.

Identifying Your Data

The point I'm trying to make is that you need to identify and analyze the type of information files you want to make available on the Internet. This decision has implications for your server type and size and for what sort of user interface to design. You will need to be able to answer the following questions for each type of information you plan to publish:

- What kind of information will you offer? Will you be making announcements, offering catalogs, posting press releases, product information, technical documents, collections of quotations, collections of photos, previews of movies, or the latest stock market quote?
- What format will you use to provide that information? Will it be plain text, formatted text, hypertext, sound, picture, video, program to be run, program to be downloaded, or something else?
- What size files will you offer?
- How generally available is the format you have selected?
- Is there a natural grouping of files – will certain files always be downloaded together?
- How often does the information in the files change?
- Who owns the information? Is copyright an issue?
- Who will update it?

- How much will you charge for it, if anything?
- What is your goal in spreading this information on the Internet?
- How will you evaluate whether you've reached that goal?

In addition, think through what happens after your server is set up. If your data are timely, you should plan to update regularly, and be sure that the date you last updated the file is a prominent feature. You will also have to think about what this means in terms of staff support.

Another part of identifying your data consists of finding and recruiting information providers, or those people or organizations that will provide you with what you plan to publish. For example, you might provide company press releases and arrange for the public relations departments to supply them to you with dates for posting and removal. You might start a literary magazine and collect short stories from high school students in your area. Or you might have a companywide telephone and e-mail directory that might be kept current by the department administrators. Be careful to verify the ownership of the files and data you publish and check for any copyright issues. Don't assume that because it's already on the Internet that it's freely available for your use.

Identifying Your Needs

Internet education can be done with little cost and time, or it can be a massive million-dollar effort.

Hardware

Given the kind of education you want to provide and the size of the audience you think you might expect, what kind of computer system is available to you to meet those needs? You can set up a server with low-powered computers, and initially that may be the quickest approach. However, if your service becomes popular, it will demand much more computing power. In either case, consider the cost as well as your familiarity with each type of hardware.

For example, you might start out with an inexpensive PC running Windows or with a Macintosh. These systems are familiar to many and are easy to set up to run Gopher or Web server software (or both in combination). This will let you get your feet wet and explore the possibilities without investing a lot of money. Or you might make space on a PC running Microsoft Windows NT. Apple sells a version of its Macintosh that is optimized to run as a WWW server. If usage exceeds the capabilities of your machine, you can move into more powerful hardware.

Note that larger, more powerful UNIX-based machines are getting easier to use. Sun Microsystems and Silicon Graphics are starting to bundle some models with Web server software and management tools to simplify server administration.

Network Connection

Do you have a dedicated Internet connection, or do you dial in for Internet access? In the latter case, you wouldn't want your home machine to be your server, because it wouldn't be available most of the time. So you'll need to determine whether Internet publishing is a service your Internet provider offers. Or you can negotiate with a service that, for a fee, will run your server on its equipment. Be sure to clarify what access you'll have for updating your information.

Software

It may be obvious to you which server (Gopher, WWW, or WAIS) or combination you want to use, but review your decision before you take the plunge. Look through (Gopher), 4 (WWW), 5 (WAIS), and 6 (Other Tools)—including the servers you don't intend to use.

Human Resources

Do you have the expertise and time in-house to comfortably run your server? Depending on the size and complexity of the computer system you'll use for your server, you may need to recruit the assistance of a system administrator. The system administrator is the person in charge of all technical aspects of running the computer system. Some of the Gopher, Web, and WAIS software discussed in this book require a system administrator to get it set up. But once it's running, the data librarian steps in. This is the person or persons who do most of the work involved in collecting, organizing, and preparing the data and documents that go on your server. They don't need much system experience at all, because the process of loading the data into the correct directories can be made quite simple. You may indeed want everyone in your organization to add and keep track of their own files on your Gopher, WWW, or WAIS server. However, you should plan to entrust someone with the overall structure and organization of your server, and that person would be the data librarian.

Make sure you have the technical support you'll need. If you plan to run a server on a system with which you are not familiar, and your system administrator is too busy to help, you should think carefully about what support you'll need and where you'll get it. Check the documentation and the newsgroup or mailing list for the type of server you plan to use to get an estimate of the technical expertise it requires. Internet server software doesn't always require a system administrator, although it's often helpful. It is possible, even preferable, to have your system administrator set up and run the server, then give control of various sections to the data owners or maintainers. In many cases, new files can be published by simply moving the files to a particular directory on the server. Remember, one goal of each of the three main server protocols, Gopher, WWW, and WAIS, was to increase the ease and access to Internet education.

What level of staff effort will be required to keep your information current? Often this isn't an issue, because you'll simply put information on your server and replace it every few months or so when it gets updated. But if your company's reputation depends on the timeliness and accuracy of the information your server provides, it would be a good idea to make sure that the burden won't be overwhelming.

Will you need the services of a graphic designer? If you're planning a WWW site, hire or consult with a graphic designer. Many Web sites show the lack of design expertise. Others use graphic design to grab your attention.

Will you need management to change policies or procedures in order to get the information and updates your server will need? Will other departments need to be involved, either in providing or using the information on your server? Will your server change some systems that are in place? Start early in recruiting management support.

Identifying Available Resources

When identifying hardware for use as a server, think about a backup. What happens if the machine breaks down? Once your server becomes established, you won't want to have any down time, planned or otherwise. The Internet is international so people will be using your server at all hours of the day and night.

Don't underestimate the time and learning involved. The kind of people you recruit should be excited and eager. This will be a learning experience for your whole crew, so be sure that they (and you) are up for it.

Determining How to Make Up the Difference

If you don't have the right computer equipment available, it's often possible to piggyback on another server. The operations can easily be separated from the user's point of view. Users often don't pay attention to which computer they are connected. Another alternative is renting time and space on a commercial service.

One advantage of Internet education is that, for the most part, it requires no specialized skill to format and prepare the information. For that reason you might include a broader range of your staff and personnel as data suppliers than you might first have expected. Ideally, the author of each document can be responsible for putting it on your server and keeping it current.

Identifying Charging Mechanisms

How to charge for information—if at all—is an area that is changing rapidly. First, I'd like to make a case for providing some real content or information on your server for free. You don't have to give away your product to be part of the Internet community, but try to offer more than just advertising and order forms. You may well find that by putting up detailed and useful information, you increase your business in other ways.

Microsoft provides access to much of its technical support Knowledge Base via the Web although it also sells the information on CD-ROM or you might use your company's server to sponsor a community organization or just provide information about your area as a gesture of community support. Some companies have offered specialized services, such as mortgage calculation or an index to 800 numbers.

But if you absolutely have to charge, some techniques are in use and others are in the advanced planning or testing stages. This is an area that is changing rapidly, so pay close attention to the sites and discussion groups you find that deal with this. Chapter 7 describes and summarizes the different approaches available.

Identifying Security Risks

Methods exist for limiting access to all or part of your server from certain Internet subnets. Be aware of this possibility when laying out your server, because you might want some sections to be available only to those on your system and others to be available to everyone. However, whenever you screen out IP addresses or subnets, you should be aware of the gateway chaining problem. Basically, this means that any gateways (for example, proxy, caching, and e-mail) to your Gopher, Web, or WAIS server should block out the same IP addresses that your server restricts. Otherwise you're leaving a back door open.

The extent to which security is an issue for you depends on the nature of your organization and computer system. For high security you could put up a firewall to protect the rest of your network from unwanted intrusion. A firewall is a method of isolating your company's or organization's computers behind a computer that acts as a gatekeeper, or firewall. All outgoing requests for information or services go to that one machine, which hides the sender's machine address but passes on the request.

For lower security you still must ensure against unauthorized alteration of your server files and operating system. Several software developers for Gopher, WWW, and WAIS have already started posting detailed analyses of their server software's security holes and risks, as well as their recommendations.

Estimating Your Costs

Like anything else, what you will spend depends on what you want to do and, in this case, how many people will come to see what you've done (i.e., browse your Gopher, Web, or WAIS server). Many people mistakenly assume that because dial-up Internet-browsing accounts can cost as little as $15 per month, Internet-publishing accounts are just as inexpensive. The type of Internet access account needed to do what's described in this book is much more expensive, sometimes running hundreds or even thousands of dollars per month, with additional hardware and line installations adding to the cost. That higher price has to do with the types of service available in your area and the Internet throughput (size of the pipeline) you'll need.

The Gopher, WWW, WAIS, or other server software you may use varies widely in price as well. Some of it is available for free, and other programs cost $5,000 to $15,000 plus annual maintenance charges of $1,000 or more. The free software may not be such a bargain when you factor in programming and debugging time.

The type of computer you use will also be an expense, but thankfully there is a movement toward using less expensive PCs and Macintoshes in the place of the larger, more support-intensive UNIX machines. Staff support costs are often underestimated.

Planning the Presentation of Your Data

A dedicated individual, or a team of editorial consultants, graphic artists, and programmers, can develop a sophisticated well-organized information server. Christine Quinn, Stanford University's director of electrical engineering for computer and network services, describes Stanford's attempts to put a consistent "Stanford" face on its collection of Web servers in an article titled "From Grass Roots to Corporate Image—The Maturation of the Web," which she presented at the 1994 WWW conference in Chicago. Because Stanford was looking for a unifying theme, the university hired a graphic artist to insert pictures of Stanford's famous architecture in its home pages.

Dale Dougherty of O'Reilly and Associates, publishers of UNIX administration books, describes Internet education as a collaborative art. At the 1994 WWW conference in Chicago he recalled how his company's extremely popular *Global Network Navigator (GNN)* site needed more editorial and production people than technical staffers. Having a graphic artist on board was essential. According to Dougherty, a publisher "organizes an audience," and educating on the Internet has the same requirements of any publishing enterprise:

- Editorial requirements include a point of view, goals, the writing and editing of new material and updating of old material.
- Strong graphics allow the publisher to create an identity—"define our space," Dougherty says.
- Technical requirements are constantly changing and not to be ignored—publishers do so at their peril.
- Business requirements include paying attention to costs. If they are high, subscriptions and advertising can defray the expense, just as they do for print.
- Sales and marketing techniques may be different but remain essential.

Even the presentation of your menus and the design of your hypertext require consideration. Are your users quickly finding the information they want from your server, or are they getting sidetracked by confusing menus?

How the information is presented--known on the Net as the metaphor that is used—can make a big difference in how easily and quickly newcomers learn their way around your information server. A metaphor is a way to describe the information server or how it is arranged by comparing it with something commonly understood. For example, a directory structure is often described as treelike, with a root and many branches. A book is another metaphor; although a book can be emulated in hypertext and has certain advantages, the flexibility of Internet servers may lead to even easier ways to organize information.

The structure of your organization might provide an obvious structure for your server, but you may prefer a more subject-oriented model based on the main areas your server covers. Here are some examples:

- If a company is composed of different divisions, its server might be split up that way as well, with branches leading off to areas that represent each division.
- If a company is global, the server might have links leading to the different geographic regions and then to the countries (and company offices) within those regions.
- If a company or organization offers a variety of services or functions, it could split its Gopher or Web server along those lines.

Extensive testing is one of the best ways to make your server and data presentation user friendly. By testing I mean trying out all the links and menus yourself from a variety of browser programs. And keep testing once your server is in use. Links can die or change on you—that link you thought was fascinating and pertinent two months ago may have changed focus or moved to another site. Also test your server's presentation by asking novice users to explore it, and then ask them to summarize what your server contains. You might be surprised by what they miss.

Always keep in mind that users are a resource. They can provide helpful information. On the Internet the bias is toward criticism and feedback (with the assumption that you'll fix what's wrong), so take advantage of that, as well as the ideas your users may provide. In their travels through the Internet they may have come across a design or presentation solution that could be useful to you. Don't forget that they may have seen and used many more servers than you have. Actually, it's common to borrow techniques from others on the Internet.

Another method is to try different approaches to presenting the same data and then use your system's logs to determine which route browsers use most.

Different people tend to learn in different ways. Psychology tells us that people have four basic learning styles:

- Reflective people relate everything to their own experience: why would I educate on the Internet?
- Conceptual people want to know the big picture: what is the significance of Internet education?

- Practical people seek usable information: how do I do it?
- Creative people are easily bored and tend to learn by trial and error: what if ?

Keep these styles in mind when designing your server. It might behoove you to present your crucial information in several different ways. For example, you could present a single concept with a written explanation, a diagram, a step-by-step example, and a discussion of the benefits and implications. Cater to the different types of learners in your audience.

Preparing Your Data

Gopher servers generally need less data preparation than WWW and WAIS servers. Usually, you just pop the file in place and it's instantly available on your server. But even with Gopher servers many questions come up about the preparation of material.

Acquiring the Material

You should analyze the need for

- Scanning in text and images from paper copies
- Optical character recognition
- Uploading existing files to your server

Formatting the Material

Formatting concerns include

- Whether to crop or edit images (retouch the boss's picture?)
- Whether to translate materials to a different format
- Which text formats to make available (for example, WordPerfect 5.1, Word for Windows 2.0, PostScript, and so on)
- Whether those formats exclude use of those files on other types of computers, such as Macintosh, UNIX, VAX, and IBM mainframe
- Whether to append a company logo, copyright statement, or author and date (can this be done automatically?)

Access to the Material

In determining which image file formats to use, you should ask whether

- Accepted standards exist for the machines you plan to use
- Your data need to be indexed, filtered, or generally cleaned up

Future

You also need to consider your needs in the future:

- Can indexing and cleanup be handled automatically by scripts or programs?
- Do you need to convey information that isn't yet standard on the Internet, such as tables and formulas that aren't easy to format on Web servers using HTML 2.0?
- Is there any provision for removing information that becomes dated?
- In what ways might the size of your server grow?

Indexing Your Data

You might consider indexing the contents of your Gopher and WWW servers (WAIS servers have built-in indexing), although it's not required or even always necessary. If you have just a few documents and your menus aren't very deep, users are unlikely to get lost or miss items on your server. However, if you have an extensive menu structure, a large collection of documents, or large documents, you should consider an index. The usual practice is to place a search link at the beginning of your opening screen that offers users the chance to search the contents of your Gopher or WWW server. Users then can search quickly through the index for what they want, instead of working their way through various submenus or hypertext links.

If you've ever been unable to find something on a server that you knew was there, you'll appreciate what a convenience the ability to search the contents of a server can be. Jughead, developed by Rhett "Jonzy" Jones, a programmer at the University of Utah, is one tool available for indexing UNIX Gopher server menus.

You also can index the full text of documents on your Gopher and WWW servers. Full-text indexing is different than indexing by menu item or file name. Full-text indexing means that every word in each document is indexed, not just the menu description line (for Gopher servers). For example, if you have a document summarizing the history of the conflict in the Middle East and it mentions Syria, the menu line might say only "Middle Eastern Conflict—History." Someone searching for everything she can find about Syria won't turn up that document. But with full-text indexing a search on *Syria* would retrieve it. Some Gopher and WWW servers, such as GN, WN, TurboGopher, and MacHTTPD, offer the ability to do full-text indexing. Others allow links to WAIS to accomplish this.

You'll want to think about what kinds of searches your users might make and whether you'll need sophisticated indexing features such as structured field searching, which means that users can search fields or certain parts of the text, including title, author, and date. Free WAIS adds structured field searching to the freeWAIS indexing software, which is available for UNIX systems. Libraries and large databases will want this level of sophistication. Whenever the text information you are publishing is so big that searching on a simple word or words fails to narrow the field, you need to consider whether fields are available and field searching is necessary.

Menu and full-text indexing are not the only kinds of indexing. If you plan to provide a large number of non-text files, such as programs, pictures, sound, and video, you will want to index them. You might index only their file names (or menu items), but if you have explanatory blurbs about each one, you will want to index the explanations so that indexes retrieve the non-text file as well.

External indexers are usually programs that attempt to go out and collect information from all over the world and then make that index available from one server. Veronica (for Gopher sites) and Archie (for FTP and Gopher sites) are the most famous examples of external indexers. External indexers are a crucial element in indexing Gopher and Webspace (Webspace means the content of all the servers browsable with WWW browsers). They are analogous to listing a book in an international card catalog system. WWW Worm (WWWW), ALIWEB (Archie-like Web), and assorted other search programs traverse the Web to develop similar indexes. Learning the techniques and philosophies behind each of these external indexers is quite useful. Sometimes you'll find theoretical papers discussing search strategies, but usually you can learn their approach within a few minutes. Then you should register your server with all those indexes that you deem appropriate if you want your server to be truly internationally available.

Indexing has many advantages for both you and your users. It can lessen the load on your server and ease the frustration and complaints users have about getting lost in large servers. But indexing can be difficult to install and complicates server administration, one responsibility of which is ensuring that the indexes are always up to date.

Registering or Announcing Your Server

Gopher, WWW, and WAIS all have free central registries that attempt to keep track of all the servers in the world. You should register with them and apprise them of any server name changes you make. You also should be aware of the subject indexes and automatic and voluntary indexing servers. Register with them as appropriate.

If your server performs a service or acts as a resource for a certain population on the Internet, post information about it to the relevant Usenet newsgroup and e-mail the appropriate mailing list. Keep your announcement short and to the point, and try to avoid boasting. Asking for feedback and additional links is both good netiquette and good business – it will help you improve your server. Finally, contact other similar Web, Gopher, and WAIS sites and invite them to link into your server. The easiest way to find related sites is to search the Internet directories and indexes using terms that describe your own server.

Maintaining Reliability

A reachable site is a well-maintained site. You should plan to budget for maintenance and hardware sufficient to handle the load. If your Gopher, WWW, or WAIS server is often down, unavailable, or filled with links that don't work or data that are out of date, your company's reputation could be hurt. Servers go down because of power failures, machine malfunctions, software bugs, human error (someone turns it off), and overload. Although nothing is fail-safe, you need to plan for monitoring and maintenance of the server hardware and software. Some sites set up automatic programs that let them know if their server is down.

Links can be incorrect if they were entered incorrectly and never checked or they changed without notification. A server has no way of knowing all the sites that link to it, so posting notices of changes to everyone who needs them is impossible, although some server administrators attempt to notify all sites they are aware of. Obviously, this requires a certain amount of personal attention. Plan to regularly verify and update your server's data and links.

You should consider mirroring to another site or backup server if you expect to have a popular server. There are actually several kinds of mirroring. One type negotiates with another site to maintain a duplicate of its site or service. These sites are often on different continents to ease the load on international links but all sites offer the same data.

In another mirroring arrangement one site maintains several machines in parallel, each acting as the Gopher or WWW server. This is what the University of Minnesota Gopher crew had to do to handle the extreme load on its Mother Gopher server in parallel, each with an 80MB hard disk just to support the top level of its Gopher server. Below that the university has a variety of machines, including Sun Microsystems and NeXT workstations and more A/UX machines.

Evaluating Server Performance and Audience Response

Evaluation is an important but often ignored component of any process. In this case most of the servers come with some sort of log file, which is easily activated if not so easily analyzed. Gopher, WWW, and WAIS servers detail what is possible with those servers, but check to see whether this information can be gleaned from the log file:

- The number of connections your server supports per hour, day, week, or month.
- Origins of connections. This shows up in the logs as host names or subnet addresses of those making connections.
- Items accessed most often.

Turning log files into useful reports is sometimes more difficult than you'd expect, and some utilities have been written to simplify this process. Because Gopher, Web, and WAIS servers routinely log the host name (and IP address) of each user's computer, along with the items retrieved, you do need to be aware of the potential for invading users' privacy. To protect users' privacy many log analysis programs automatically strip off the lowest level of IP address in their reports, which removes this link to individuals. You need to know who your audience is, but you don't need to know who each user is. You might also consider modifying the server software to remove the link between users and items retrieved.

Nothing prevents you from building your own evaluation tools into your server. For example, some servers allow users to fill out a questionnaire. The answers can be stored in a private file, e-mailed directly to you, or posted right back on your server. One WWW site has a "sign-in sheet" that allows users to leave a comment as well as their name and e-mail address, data then added automatically to what is displayed on the server. Be aware that not all browsers support online forms, so always give your users an alternative, such as a way to e-mail their comments.

Another option is to provide users with a voice telephone number, fax number, e-mail address, and/or postal address from which they may obtain further information. Although this somewhat defeats the purpose of education on the Internet, responses can be an objective measure of the interest generated by your server.

Or perhaps you've posted a catalog, and users place their orders through an existing telephone or fax order system. In that case make sure that the order form or telephone operator asks for the source of users' information, so that you can accurately evaluate your server's contribution.

Using What You've Learned

You may or may not have planned to implement your Gopher, WWW, or WAIS server in stages, but almost certainly you will learn from the process and find better ways to accomplish your goals. Given that this is a most malleable medium, you should plan to continually check, revise, update, and perhaps redesign your server.

It is an artificial restriction to say that once it's up it can't be changed. That logic may apply to print versions, but with the Internet there's no such thing as final.

However, if you change information or remove menus that may have been linked by other servers, you should post explanatory notes. In such cases it is helpful to leave a link in place that describes the change and gives the new link information. You may also find it helpful to keep an administrator's log, describing the changes you make to software and hardware and particularly any changes in philosophy on menu arrangement or hypertext design. Also record any addition of other resources, such as a searchable index or major bodies of information, such as new departments. You may find the log useful in the future, or it may give another administrator an insight into your server's design. Much of this is of interest to your users as well, so you should consider adding a "What's New" section to your server for providing this information online. If you do, you should still keep a separate and private administrator's log in which you record changes or upgrades in your system or server software as well as problems you encounter and their solutions.

Summary

This chapter is about the groundwork you should do before you start providing education on the Internet. This includes exploring Gopher, Web, and WAIS sites both in your subject area and in others to get ideas and techniques you can use in your server. And keep notes of the problems you have and what helped and didn't help in your searches.

You will need to answer many questions—about your audience, your competition, charging policies, and how the information you publish will be gathered as well as maintained. You may need to think about a graphic designer. Are there any special security issues?

The presentation and organization of your data can be an important factor in your site's success. Do you have a design team or will you need one? Think about indexing the contents of your server wherever you have a large amount of material. Both internal and external indexes are important, so be sure to register your server.

Also plan for continual maintenance and testing of your server's links. They can go out of date quickly, but tools are available to help you do the testing automatically.

Evaluate your server log files, particularly the error logs. Ask for feedback from your users (by e-mail, online forms, or even phone or fax). Users are a resource; don't waste them. This is a growing medium, so assume that your server will need to be redesigned regularly, that it is a perpetual work in progress.

Finally, remember that the Internet is not just millions of potential customers; it's also a network of people with varied interests, enthusiasms, and talents. Contribute something to the Internet to help it grow.

4

Benefits for Internet Learning

Information technologies might improve learning and teaching in two distinct ways. Just as they have made workers more productive in business and commerce, they could reduce teaching costs or increase the speed with which learners acquire knowledge. Alternatively, such technologies might help improve the quality of learning, rather than simply making it faster and cheaper. In this section we first review evidence that information technologies can improve the efficiency of learning and teaching; then we consider how they might lead to better educational outcomes.

Reducing Costs and Increasing Productivity

Most discussions of computers in education look at how new technologies might improve "instruction delivery," a management theorist's way of saying how teachers teach and how learners learn. Therefore, as resources for higher education continue to dwindle, when most people think of information technologies, it will usually be in terms of how such technologies might reduce the number of teachers needed or cut the time (and money) it takes learners to acquire skills. A collection of cases in current practice suggests that some technologies do indeed help improve productivity in these ways.

Current successes are subject to several qualifications. Some cost savings are modest, others come with hidden prices (for example, high development costs or lower graduation rates), and all depend on careful attention to implementation in the classroom. But, although the data are still unclear, the economic logic behind the view is relatively straightforward: Cut costs by doing more with less; that is, hold student outcomes roughly constant (or improving) while displacing labor (staff) with capital (here, information technology). With technology costs continually dropping while labor costs only rise, this trade-off appears a good one for increasing productivity.

Site/Study	*Cost-Effectiveness Results*
Computer-Aided Instruction (CAI) and Computer-Based Instruction (CBT)	
Orlansky and String (1979)	-30 percent reduction in time to achieve criterion performance using computer-based
instruction	in military training
Fletcher (1991)	-30 percent time savings, 30-40 percent cost savings, and improved achievement using multimedia instruction
Levin (1989)	-CAI proved more cost-effective than reducing class size or extending length of school day -but less effective than peer tutoring
Hall (1995) training compared based	-CBT in business reduced time 40 to 80 percent with traditional text- training
	-CBT in business reduced training costs 40 to 85 percent compared with traditional training
Roberts (1991)	-IBM cut its annual training budget (over $1 billion) by $30 million by using CBT

Intelligent Tutoring Systems (ITS)	
U.S Air Force	-ITS traditionally deliver high student learning outcomes, but at a high price; the Air Force aims to cut development costs by 95 percent and development time by up to 80 percent -the result would be an overall reduction in training costs
Distance Learning	
Open University, United Kingdom (1989)	-cost per graduate lower than conventional university's
Deakin University, Australia (1989)	-cost per student 97 percent that of on-campus student
Indira Gandhi National Open University, India (1991)	-cost per student between 8 and 40 percent of cost at conventional university -student performance rates only 60 percent
Open University teacher training, Indonesia (1988)	-cost per student about 60 percent of cost at conventional university
Everyman University, Israel (1978)	-cost per graduate estimated at one-half cost at conventional university
Teacher training at a distance, Tanzania (1979/1984)	-costs about one-half those at a conventional university
National Technological University, USA (1989)	-break-even point (in per-student cost) at 9,000 students in 200 courses

Figure 4-1: Information Technology and Cost Savings

CAI and CBT

Computer-aided instruction (CAI) and computer-based training (CBT) have shown some ability to do more with less, by providing learners drill-and-practice systems that replace teachers in routine coaching tasks. These systems are most frequently found in secondary schools but also play a role in remedial math, science, and language courses at the collegiate level, as well as in business and military training. However, as convenient as they might be for self-paced learning, CBT programs often do not yield dramatic cost savings. Development costs for multimedia courseware are usually very high, often offsetting savings in delivery, and the price of a stand-alone computer system for each student is sometimes so dear that labor costs must fall dramatically before any net savings appears. The latter situation may change in the future, however, as powerful machines drop roughly to the cost of a top-of-the-line TV.

Distance Learning

A few intelligent tutoring systems (ITS) also have reported cost-reductions in training. But, as with CAI and CBT, development costs currently impose strong limits on their productivity gains. In fact, the main attraction of ITS is that they may improve the quality of learning rather than reduce costs, as we discuss later under "Increasing Quality and Productivity."

Today, distance learning whereby students and teachers rely on electronic and hardcopy media, rather than on face-to-face contact, for at least some of their communication (correspondence courses by postal mail are perhaps the oldest form of distance learning)- provides probably the best examples of cost savings that are at least partly attributable to information technologies. In this country, the PLATO system, among others, pioneered distance learning in the 1960s, connecting as many as one thousand student-terminals at a time to mainframes. Several studies show that distance-learning courses in Asia cost from 45 to 90 percent of the cost of conventional college classes, with comparable student performance; costs can drop to as little as 8 percent of on-campus courses, although completion rates then also seem to dip. Using telecommunications to offer distance learning for over three decades, the Open University in Great Britain — one of the first very large-scale experiments in distance learning at the higher education level — boasts average per-student costs of around one half those of conventional campuses.) We briefly examine its success to show why, at least right now, distance learning can help reduce costs only under relatively narrow circumstances.

The Open University. An Example in Achieving Cost Reductions. First, the technology must allow many students to be taught at once. Class sizes at the Open University usually exceed 200. The larger the

> *The best-known example in higher education, and most successful example of its kind in the world, is the UK Open University. Some 40 distance teaching institutions across the world have been based on the OU model. It's methods are well known, but it is worth emphasizing an important aspect that is often misunderstood. Although the OU has developed widely admired methods for the use of teams in the design and production of teaching resources, mainly paper-based materials, and although it still carries in many people's minds the image of the "University of the Air," it is the UK-wide network of part-time tutors who provide the main teaching that is experienced by OU students. Tutorial support is provided by traveling to quite frequent face-to-face meetings, by telephone contact, and by feedback on written assignments. In a real sense, the formal aspects of studying for an OU degree differ little from those experienced by students on a conventional campus. The cost per student, however, is about one-half that of conventional campus universities. The OU is now exploring how best to build on its success through the emerging advanced learning technology (ALT), in particular the use of CMC (computer-mediated communication) for collaborative learning and the delivery of its course materials through CD-ROM.*

Class size, the greater the student-teacher ratio, which lowers labor costs and spreads high development and initial technology costs, leading, in turn, to productivity improvements. Break-even points -class sizes for which the cost of distance education and traditional delivery are roughly equal — will vary depending on, among other things, the size of technology investment and the course being taught. But it is a safe bet, at least for the near term, that distance learning classes of less than 20 will rarely lead to substantial per student cost reductions.

Second, a substantial amount of labor must be displaced by technology. Typically, labor is over 95 percent the cost of the class; so, modest trades of faculty for machines will not substantially change overall prices. Consequently, distance learning works best in relatively "standard" courses – math and the sciences – for which knowledge is relatively routine, can be embedded in the technology, and can have much teaching delegated to it. Alternatively, to expand the range of courses that can be taught at a distance, the use of technology should be carefully designed so that expensive labor at least can be replaced by cheaper help. For example, the Open University makes liberal use of tutors (replacing many full professors), either in person or on the phone.

Third, technology should substitute for labor as simply as possible. As the example of the Open University suggests, most low-cost distance learning does not fundamentally change the learning experience for the student, or the teacher. A computer application that promised to play a substantial role in teaching but that also demanded broad changes in faculty skills and activities could actually increase labor costs, even while guaranteeing a savings in teacher time.

The bottom line, then, is that today's distance-learning technology is largely limited to imparting relatively routine skills and knowledge, taught *en masse,* through relatively traditional methods. Most of the best examples actually come from military and corporate training, rather than from higher education. For example, large companies such as Ford now contract for distance instruction to help their employees learn how to use tools such as spreadsheets and word processors, as well as specialized equipment. And Hewlett-Packard estimates that it saves millions of dollars each year using distance learning to train employees more effectively and more efficiently than with conventional methods. These examples explain why well over one-half of distance learning now goes on not in academic settings but in businesses – a market that is expanding so rapidly that whole TV networks are now dedicated to corporate distance learning.

The Internet is increasingly being viewed as a medium that can bring distance learning and its cost benefits into the higher-education sector. In the next subsection, we look at the cost and other advantages the Internet in particular can provide as a distance-learning tool for higher-education institutions.

Internet Impact: Distance Learning, Cost Reduction, and Increased Access

At least partly to cut costs, almost all higher-education institutions in the United States are considering distance-learning programs, dozens already have substantial offerings in place, and many universities are now moving in this direction. In the future, we believe that the Internet will be the most cost-effective way to deliver a new generation of distance-learning courses. By winter 1996, the U.S. Distance Learning Association listed many dozens of universities with homepages outlining their WWW and Internet-based courseware. At the same time, the World Lecture Hall, a Web site managed by the University of Texas, has become a "virtual repository," organizing links to hundreds of other sites that are making Web-based class materials available to anyone who is interested.

Because the WWW first came online only in 1991, all these courses are new, and there are no solid data proving the effectiveness of Internet-based distance education. But a chemistry curriculum drawn almost at random from the World Lecture Hall illustrates some of the reasons why Web-based distance learning seems very promising, at least "on paper". To begin with, emerging Internet courses can include a wealth of material about the class (lectures, exams, assignments) and references to relevant online literature (books, programs, tools such as the periodic table), all accessible at the click of a mouse on a hypertext link. Each of these sources can be constructed as multimedia documents, including pictures, digitized audio versions of lectures, presentation overheads – even simulations, which can be run to give a much more dynamic impression of processes and structures. Full high bandwidth interactivity will be available soon, to support multi-person, multimedia dialogues in real-time. The new generation of Chemistry 22C is taught by Prof. James C. Baird of Brown University. The WWW course materials, found indexed under "Chemistry" on the World Lecture Hall, include

- online lecture notes
- lecture "overheads"
- digitized audio of actual lectures, which can be played, rewound, replayed
- homework assignments and answers, updated weekly
- electronic archives of past final exams and answers
- pointers to online resource material.

Students access these different resources just as they do any Web homepage: by pointing and clicking on text links.

While this example is quite complete, it did not include features found in a few other course homepages:

- ***Calendar of class sessions:*** Often presented as a table, including date of the class and daily topic. The topic description is often hypertext; clicking on it allows access to the material for the class (lectures, overheads, etc.).
- ***Virtual office hours:*** Some professors included buttons thatallowed students to send e-mail to them or to other students in the class.
- ***"Chat" rooms:*** In some classes, students can login and engage in text-based discussions with other students from the class who also happen to be on at the same time. Faculty also often pre- arrange virtual office hours: times at which they will be logged-on as well.
- ***Video and movie clips:*** Video clips (usually less than a minute in duration, given current time and space constraints) are sometimes included in Web courseware to demonstrate complex physical processes, for example.
- ***"Live" computer programs:*** In an increasing number of Web-based courses, students can run simulations, in addition to *viewing static lecture materials.* The simulations run on remote machines, but display on the user's machine, and often permit the student to interact with the simulation and control its execution - for instance, using forms to input simulation parameters.

Figure 4-2: Internet-Based Distance Learning: Today and Tomorrow

Internet-based distance-learning courses, in short, can mix the graphics and video of instructional TV with a much more intimate style of interactive mentoring than teleconferencing ever could. Therefore, it should provide substantially richer learning experiences for students than the current generation does.

Web-based distance learning might enhance productivity in higher education in several ways. Most obviously, by providing a more powerful and flexible medium, the Web should enable developers to construct higher-quality courseware for a wider range of classes than ever before. With richer courseware, classes for which computers once replaced only a modest amount of labor might shortly be taught almost exclusively through technology; and in courses in which information technology previously had no part, it may play at least a supporting role. All this means that Web based learning tools, appropriately used, promise to replace more labor and, consequently, to lower faculty costs.

But less-visible features of Internet-based distance learning – costs and standards – may enhance productivity even more dramatically. It is reasonable to assume that if courseware built on the Web is richer than previous distance-learning products, it might also be more costly to deliver – reasonable, but probably wrong. Although few realize it, the Internet is not only a better medium for learning and interaction but a *cheaper* way to deliver instruction – something providers of corporate training have already figured out. For example, corporate providers are quickly trading their old on-demand video systems for more-flexible and less-expensive high-capacity intranets, which use Internet-style communication on private networks to deliver full-motion video to hundreds of viewers at once, at the click of a mouse.

Schools and homes can expect similar benefits, even if they cannot afford the high-capacity LANs of big business. High-bandwidth yet low-cost connections to the WWW will soon come in several forms. Many homes today can access the Internet cheaply through ISDN phone connections, providing about 5 to 10 times the effective bandwidth of ordinary phone lines. More interestingly, successful trials of cable modems in 1996 promise very high-speed Internet connections, at roughly the cost of standard cable service. The Internet's promise for distance learning is based on its potential to provide a flexible and high-functionality medium for delivering instruction, at a cost that is now within reach and steadily dropping.

The powerful functionality is based on several features:

- ***Two-way interactive communication.*** The Internet supports distance learning, whereby students communicate with teachers (or technology), as easily as it enables learning where teachers communicate to students. Generally, students learn better from interactive courseware than from one-way instruction. Of course, if desired, TV-style distance-learning lectures can readily be simulated on the Internet.
- *On-demand communication protocol.* Courseware is accessed on the Internet whenever the user wants it, and from wherever the student plugs in his or her machine. No need to remember when an instructional show is on, or even to set the VCR.
- *Wide communication bandwidth.* Recent advances in compression, coupled with innovative ways to use existing infrastructure (new modems that transform TV cable into full-duplex computer connections, and ISDN as well as ADSL for copper phone wire) will make roughly the capacity of two-way video available to most Internet users.

Costs are dropping for several reasons:

- *Hardware needed for Internet access is dropping quickly in price.* In 1995 Web access required at least a low-end PC; less than two years later, "Internet appliances" such as WebTV permit Web surfing at about the cost of a television plus monthly cable charges
- *Network costs are dropping to zero.* Or, more precisely, the cost of using the Internet is low and independent of distance, so it should be just as cheap to access distance-learning material from New Zealand as from next door. (This is why more and more people are using the Internet for their telephone service, to the consternation of long-distance phone companies.)
- *De facto standards are making it easier to develop sharable courseware.* The WWW is rooted in a few document and communication protocols to which most homepage builders (or, more generally, publishers) currently adhere to.

Figure 4-3: Is the Internet the Medium of Choice for Distance Learning?

Video on the Internet

In some ways, Web TV resembles on-demand video systems thatsome companies already use for training videos and inspirationalmessages from above. Indeed, it might even be better. One failing of corporate video systems has been the need for a user to download the video from an archival computer (known as a server), store it on the receiving computer (the client), and then "decompress" it before being able to play it back with special viewing software – a process taking anything from ten minutes to a few hours. With Web TV it should be possible simply to click and watch.

Figure 4-4: The Internet As a Higher-Functionality

If this promise is realized, the much-heralded-but never-accomplished "500 channels of cable TV" finally could turn into something really useful. And, because they require no new and costly infrastructure development, wireless connections, such as

Cable Modem Trial Deemed Successful

A marketing trial of high-speed cable modem service conducted by Time Warner subsidiary Paragon Cable has shown virtually no churn among its 200 test participants and the waiting list is still about 300 customers long. "There's a real business here," concludes Paragon's general manager. Elmira, NY, cable customers paid a $30 installation charge and a $25 fee to receive Zenith modem units that provided access to a local database and to the Internet. Building on their success, Paragon plans to take the service commercial in Elmira at the end of March, and Time Warner is scouting out other likely locations for pilot programs.

Figure 4-5: Internet Access at the Cost of Cable TV Connection

Direct PC may be the most promising of all. In short, the technical problems facing the installation of inexpensive wide-bandwidth Internet connections are all but solved; the policy barriers, however, loom large.

In addition to reducing educational costs, the shrinking price of delivering Internet-based distance learning should help address other challenges for higher education. For one thing, Internet-based distance learning could be conveniently accessible to many different kinds of learners. Part of this improved access simply means putting more people in touch with more learning resources. A new wave of cheap "Internet appliances" (dumb terminals dedicated to Web browsing) should bring Internet access within almost anyone's budget and once on the Internet, all resources are equally inexpensive to browse, whether they happen to be on a homepage next door or thousands of miles away. Equally important for improved access is the ability of Internet distance learning to reach consumers at any place and any time. This flexibility will be especially important, for example, to workers who want to "retool" skills at night while working during the day.

Reflection: The Death of Distance as a Barrier to Learning

At the broadest level, an Internet style of learning or instruction delivery will, we believe, be so common that it makes little sense to view distance learning as a special form of education delivery. Since Internet and Web tools will continue to drop in cost and increase in functionality for the foreseeable future, technology should, over time, displace more and more faculty labor. Further, what labor cannot be displaced will at least not have to be nearby: The Internet can connect students with faculty and peers as easily as it connects learners with multimedia documents. Eventually, then, most learning will be distance-independent, and the special cases will be those that are geographically bound.

Perhaps more to the point, distance learning should be viewed as a common tool in higher education, not as a separate and esoteric -option. And most courses should be designed to use distance learning in some capacity, and often in a variety of capacities. A wide range of experiments in distance learning are already under way, and they come in many forms, rather than all fitting one mold. The degree to which direct interactions are replaced can vary significantly: Telecommunications are sometimes little more than an add-on to classroom lectures; conversely, taped lectures may be the centerpiece of instruction, with face-to-face tutoring serving as a supplement; in still other cases, all discussion happens at a distance.

There is no single, obvious way to order courses from light to heavy users of distance-learning technology. Some courses that are, for example, offered exclusively at a distance (no face-to-face interaction) still make less use of telecommunication connections than classes that also include some direct contact. We ordered the following list roughly from courses that provide narrow connectivity, overall, to those that provide rich interactions.

Less obviously, examples also differ in the bandwidth of communication, as well as the degree of interactivity. Early distance-learning courses (through postal mail) trafficked only in text, and a single interchange required days, if not weeks – not at all interactive by today's standards. Videotaped lectures distributed from a centralized source offer much greater bandwidth but no more interactivity; on the other hand, e-mail discussions between teachers and students are highly interactive but narrow in bandwidth. Some of the newest Internet-based distance learning (enjoys both broadband, multimedia connections and real-time interactions, often linking not only faculty with students, but students with one another and with shared online resources. While earlier distance-learning models delivered knowledge from a centralized teacher (or "server") to students through narrow, slow, and separate connections, newer models look.

Features and Functionality	*Examples*
low bandwidth, non-interactive technology; no face-to-face contact	Pittman's correspondence courses on shorthand in the 1840s
high bandwidth, non-interactive technology; no face-to-face contact	The Teaching Company video and audio tapes, augmented by written course material
low- to mid-bandwidth, non-interactive technology; some face-to-face contact	early courses from the Open University, mainly based on paper materials, and telephone and face-to-face tutoring
high-bandwidth, non-interactive technology;	many corporate training courses using "Web TV" are centered on

some face-to-face contact supplements distance	on-demand (tutoring multimedia courseware, but also include on-site discussions learning)
high-bandwidth, non-	many satellite- and TV-based interactive technology;
distance- learning courses, for classes are planned around	extensive face-to-face which
interaction (distance learning supplements traditional)	regularly scheduled broadcasts some World Lecture Hall classes;

Features and Functionality	*Examples*
	courseware is put online as an adjunct
high-bandwidth, interactive technology; some face-to-face contact (tutoring supplements distance learning)	some asynchronous learning courses ; students near a campus may come to on-site tutorials
low-bandwidth, interactive technology; connectivity among students and distributed resources, as well as among teachers; no "worlds"	educational MUDs or MOOs, where collections of learners (mentors and students) engage in text-based dialogues in real-time and construct textual face-to-face contact
high-bandwidth, interactive technology; fully connected community (teachers, students, resources, and experts); no face-to-face contact (or optional)	newer Internet-based course from the Open University , where face-to-face tutoring can be replaced by online tutoring and e-mail
	many courses offered at virtual universities such as Athena much more like an electronic
community, faculty, a rich, contacts.	tying together students, and distributed tools in speedy web of digital

Figure 4-6 Many Forms of Distance Learning

With so many variants, it is no surprise that what makes an application of information technology an instance of distance learning is becoming less and less clear. For example, courseware such as the chemistry curriculum in the World Lecture Hall might be used in a distance-learning class; but right now, it is simply online material for an on-campus course. However, merely by skipping lectures and labs and relying on the rich Web documents to compensate for reduced in-person contact, individual students may turn it into a virtual distance-learning course. Such individual experiments, which probably have gone on informally for decades, now are leading to large-scale studies that will try to gauge the importance of distance as a barrier to learning in technology-intensive courses.

It is useful to view this increasing freedom from spatial location in terms of the progressive "unbundling" of teaching functions in higher education as educational technologies have changed across time. Centuries ago, when knowledge was conveyed exclusively through an oral tradition, location was everything. With the advent of written texts, students were freed from the need to attend lectures (logically, but not always legally); however, other important functions, including tutoring, counseling, and evaluation, remained essentially face-to-face activities.

The Alfred P. Sloan Foundation is funding research on asynchronous learning networks (ALN) as part of its Learning Outside the Classroom program . Courses are used by students at varying distances from campus – living on campus, within commuting distance, or very far away. Two of the questions being examined by different projects are

- How well do students learn as a function of distance from the physical classroom?
- How do students' learning practices differ as a function of distance?

Figure 4-7: Does Distance Matter in Asynchronous Learning Environments?

Now, just as books (and cars) have weakened the links between distance and learning in the past, today new information technologies can almost break them. Since the Internet can connect students with teachers as easily as it connects students with course material, tutoring and counseling can be (and are) done through e-mail and real time chat rooms. Similarly, as reference materials increasingly become available in digital form, students will no longer need proximity to libraries. Evaluation and assessment also can be done at a distance. Written products, such as essays, already are created routinely with word processors; sending them across a network for grading can be easier than printing them and walking them into a professor's office. Multiple-choice as well as short-answer tests have been computerized for years. In a pinch, even timed, closed-book exams could be conducted using simple keystroke logging or more sophisticated Internet video products such as CU-SeeMe for proctoring.

Again, the point is not that learning *should* be conducted at a distance, just that creative applications make distance less and less of a barrier to learning. The challenge will be to discover the most effective applications of distance-learning technology and to blend them together with traditional face-to-face transactions.

Increasing Quality and Productivity

While many applications of information technology in education try to reduce costs, others focus on the output side of the productivity equation: helping students learn more or better, or to learn new skills — applications rarely included in higher-education curricula. A collection of examples illustrates several ways in which information-technology applications could lead to better learning and teaching outcomes.

CAI and CBT

As discussed, most successful computer-aided instruction and computer-based training applications boast of cost reductions, but a few also claim gains in the quality of student learning. Some of these applications rely on distinctly cutting-edge technology, making lavish use of multimedia, and engaging students in highly interactive discussions. However, other ideas are surprisingly simple. For example, The Teaching Company (TTC) thinks that the videotapes and audiotapes it offers can help college students improve grades in everything from history to psychology to physics. Of course, these tapes lack the interactivity of a good tutoring session, but TTC is gambling that the quality of its tapes will more than compensate: The lectures are delivered by elite, "superstar" faculty in each field, not by merely competent professors.

Some very positive reviews of these products may be too optimistic. Computer-based applications that change learning qualitatively come in various types. We order these, very roughly, from those that help students learn concepts more effectively to applications that change the kinds of ideas students learn, and how they learn them.

System/Study	*Quantative/Qualitative Learning Results*
CAI and CBT	
Flestcher (meta-analysis of 47 studies) (1989) Kulik (review of many studies and 12 meta-analyses) (1994)	.50 standard deviations improvement in achievement (IVD technology, averaged across higher education and military training) settings (CBT technology).
The Teaching Company, http://real.org/members/listing/general/2048.22ab (video and audiotapes)(1996)	as of May 1996, mainly testimonials about dramatic learning enhancements attributable to use of " superstar" tapes
Intelligent Tutorial System	
SHERLOCK (Katz et al., 1993)	provides the equivalent of 4 years of on-the-job training in electronic troubleshooting in 20 to 30 hours
ACT tutors (1995)	30 to 60 percent faster learning of programming skilld, 30 to 40 percent higher scores on tests.
	one-grade (e.g., C to B) improvement in geometry

System/Study	*Quantative/Qualitative Learning Results*
Interactive Learning Environment	
Apple's Classrooms of Tomorrow (ACOT) schools (Dwyer, 1994)	studies show students wrote better, completed units in math more rapidly
	by the end of 4 years, students changed how they did work, freely employing inquiry, collaboration, and general problem-solving skills
Collaborative visualization project (Gomez and CoVis) Gordin, (1996)	young students were able to acquire sophisticated understanding of climate and global warming
	they were also able to use high-tech visualization tools, engage in open-ended inquiries, and learn collaboratively
Massivley parallel microworlds (Resnick, 1994)	young students were able to learn about complex distributed systems using simulation models run on parallel machines
	They were also able to learn general heuristics for modeling decentralized systems
MUDs, MOOs, and MUSEs	most results are anecdotal, but broadly, MUDs may help learning of:
multi-user real-time virtual realities; as of 1996, most still text-based chat rooms, but an increasing on the Web have graphical interfaces	academic skills (programming, reading, typing, writing)
	metacognitive and generic skills (scientific method, learning to learn, help seeking)
	personal and social skills (motivation, collaboration, trust)

Figure 4-8: Information Technology and Quality Learning

It make educational packages featuring superstar instructors easier to develop and more broadly accessible, perhaps leading to significant improvements in teaching and learning productivity. Imagine, for example, a course built around master lectures, digitized and put online, and combined with complementary assignments, projects, tutorials, and group discussions – like those already found in World Lecture Hall courses. Taking this course through the Internet might not be quite the same as being there in person, which would require being a student at MIT, Stanford, or a similarly elite and pricey institution. Nonetheless, for less-fortunate students, such an online.

The Teaching Company is a for-profit business that offers more than 60 audio and video courses on a wide range of academic subjects, from science to philosophy. Most are at the college level. Their main selling point is that lectures (the courses are in very traditional delivery formats, with little support material) are taught by a "dream team" of "superstar" teachers. Almost all have first-rank U.S. university affiliations. While The Teaching Company offers no solid evidence of student learning (in fact, they provide no tests or accreditation), they do pepper their brochures with testimonials from the likes of Ted Kennedy, Orrin Hatch, and the *Los Angeles Times*.

Figure 4-9: Online Superstar Teachers

The course could be better than an in-person course offered by a second tier university. Here, as in other areas, information technology might lead to improvements in productivity by making truly great – not merely competent – practitioners and their performances available to almost everyone.

Intelligent Tutoring Systems

While replicating outstanding teaching *performances* on video might lead to improvements in learning productivity, a much more ambitious approach is to try to capture, in software, the *reasoning* of teachers. Of course, this cannot be done just by pointing a camera at a smart talking head. Rather, the process of developing so-called intelligent tutoring systems (ITS) begins with an *expert system* — a collection of heuristic rules — that is capable of answering questions and solving problems in a given subject matter. For instance, the expert system inside a good calculus ITS would be able to solve arbitrary symbolic integration problems, and would do so in a way that approximates how an "ideal" human mathematician would reason. The expert system in an ITS is often supplemented with a student modeling capability, which can examine a student's reasoning, find the exact step at which he or she went astray, try to diagnose the reasons for the error, and even suggest ways of overcoming the impasse.

The potential value of such highly intelligent systems is obvious. Indeed, for decades, the idea of supplying students with their own automated tutor, capable of tailoring learning experiences to students' needs at a fine level, has been the holy grail of teaching technology — with good reason. Many studies have shown that one-on one tutoring is the best way to learn.

However, while such systems show that ITS can raise the output side of the productivity equation in education, their successes to date are very limited. Because they try to embed detailed human-reasoning skills, both in subject-matter areas and in teaching expertise, they rely on advances in cognitive theory and software engineering. But these disciplines have yielded a detailed understanding of thinking in only a very few well-defined subjects; consequently, ITS currently are confined to relatively simple parts of algebra, geometry, computer programming, physics, and other sciences.

In higher education, then, ITS probably would be most appropriate in basic freshman and remedial classes. And, needless to say, even in these subjects, automated tutors come nowhere near the ability to mimic superstar teachers. On the contrary, ITS are frequently called "brain damaged" by most computer scientists, their developers included. Over time, however, ITS will get smarter and smarter. Buttressed by advances in cognitive science, they will capture an increasing share of human-teaching expertise, and they will extend to a wider range of subjects.

However, all evidence suggests progress here will be slow. While the speed of computer hardware continues roughly to double every two years, the intelligence of computer software, however you measure it, creeps ahead at a snail's pace. But this does not mean that information technology is destined to play only a minor role in helping improve the quantity and quality of learning in higher education. It just means that some of the most obvious ways in which technology attempts to partially replace faculty as lecturers or tutors in a traditional classroom setting may not be the most promising ways, at least in the short run.

Interactive Learning Environments

The most successful applications of information technology follow a very different principle: Instead of mimicking human tutors, they provide rich, simulated environments that enable students or trainees to practice skills intensively. Flight simulators, the first such learning environments, are still perhaps the most compelling ones. For decades they have been singularly effective technologies for improving the quality of pilot training. In the protective environment of a virtual cockpit, pilots can perfect difficult maneuvers, trying them over and over without fear of the deadly effects of a real-world mistake.

A descendent in spirit of these early simulators, demonstrates similarly impressive outcomes: Students can learn electronics troubleshooting and fault-diagnosis skills in less than one-tenth the time they previously required. While SHERLOCK includes some important coaching supports, the basic reason that trainees acquire skills so rapidly is simply that the system can present students with simulated problem situations that arise only rarely in the real world – namely, troubleshooting the complex hardware that diagnoses faulty F-15 avionics.

Well-publicized successes of "man over machine," such as Deep Blue's recent win over world chess champion Gary Kasparov, are false counter-examples. Deep Blue's performance relied almost exclusively on fast computer hardware. The program uses brute-force searches and "understands" virtually nothing about the way humans play the game. It is just this kind of understanding that automated tutors must possess if they are to help humans learn.

Interactive and simulation-based learning environments such as those we discuss here are certainly not the only alternatives to ITS and systems that try to be "smart" or human-like.

Trainees do not learn these troubleshooting skills very quickly in the field, because problems that might foster new knowledge naturally occur, say, once every few weeks. Using SHERLOCK, such problems can be made to order every few minutes, if necessary. More generally, this and other virtual worlds rely on the fact that one of the most powerful ways to learn is by doing; but learning-by-doing works well only if the world cooperates by providing the learner with a large number of practice cases, and cases suitable to the learner's current level of expertise. In situations where the real world cannot be easily controlled or does not readily cooperate, computers can now provide rich simulated worlds, at an arbitrarily high degree of fidelity, that can be controlled with the click of a mouse.

Such environments seem promising tools for training, but can they work in higher education? While it is relatively easy to imagine how simulated worlds might be useful in teaching concrete subjects such as electronics or even physics, it is less obvious how simulations would help in abstract or symbolic disciplines such as history, philosophy, or the social sciences. However, some innovative systems are already pointing the way. True, these models do not simulate concrete physical systems; but, at an abstract level, the conceptual systems they represent also comprise dynamic cause-and-effect relationships among a collection of variables. What a new generation of simulation-based learning environments are doing, in essence, is combining computational models of such processes with highly graphical and easy-to-manipulate "visualization" front-ends. Collectively, these environments give the learner a virtual world in which many what-if experiments can be performed.

In theory, then, just as SHERLOCK provides trainees with a large number of rich avionics cases, these simulations might present learners with, say, a series of hypothetical history scenarios, some of which may have analogs in real historical events and some not. These technologies appear very interesting, but they are also very new. Whether they can lead to the dramatic gains in the quantity of learning we find with SHERLOCK remains to be seen.

Rebel! Is an interactive, exploratory simulation environment for learning history – in particular the American Revolution – by playing what-if games (e.g., "What if the British had sent over more troops?"). Using it as a stand-alone system, students start the simulation, then set certain parameters (to operationalize their questions), either by loading scenarios that define collections of values or by changing them individually. Next, the system runs, and, as simulation time steps forward, the student views the virtual world unfold in a series of graphical depictions of simulation state changes. At any point the student can interrupt the run and click interface buttons that help give a better understanding of cause and effect: what was happening, and hy. We transformed *Rebel!* from an isolated simulation (running and displaying on the same machine) into a distributed one (running on a *remote* machine, and displaying on a *local* one) using the following procedure.

- The initial homepage shows, on the local interface, a picture of the initial *Rebel!* Interface (saved as a GIF file, referenced in the HTML code for the page).
- The initial page also includes a Begin button, which, when clicked, triggers a script that causes *Rebel!* to begin running on the remote machine; it also invokes a new HTML page – the initialization page.
- The initialization page allows the user to select from pre-existing scenarios and to set values for specific parameters. When the form is complete, the user clicks the Run button. This invokes a script that ships all the initialization data back to the remote machine, where the *Rebel!* process is waiting for it. On the remote machine, the simulation parameter values set by the user on the local machine are then read in, and the remote *Rebel!* Simulation run actually starts.
- As the simulation runs, it periodically updates its state and writes (actually, creates on the fly) a new HTML document (representing the simulation state), and puts it into the *output file,* to be displayed on the student's local machine.
- HTTP protocol on the local machine polls the remote machine at regular intervals, looking for an updated interface document in the output file, and loads it when necessary.

- "Stop" is always one option on each reloaded document. If the student selects the Stop button, a script writes instructions to a user *input file* on the remote machine, which causes the remote simulation to suspend.
- Throughout the run, a similar protocol enables the user on the local machine to interact with the simulation on the remote one: the simulation always looks for messages in the user input file to modulate its behavior, and the Web browser on the local machine always updates its image of the simulation interface by reloading the simulation output file.

Figure 4-10: Transforming *Rebel!* from an Isolated Application to a Web Distance-Learning Tool

Internet Impact: Stand-AlOne Systems into Cheaper Distance-Learning Technologies

Some of the applications that promise to help raise educational productivity by improving student learning, rather than by cutting costs, are already network-based systems. In CoVis, for example, students use the Internet to communicate with distant mentors, collaborate on projects with peers, gather data from remote sites, and talk with experts in atmospheric and environmental sciences. But many of the cutting-edge applications are stand-alone systems that run on only one or a few computer platforms. For instance, one might work on a Macintosh but not on a PC. Even worse, since many of these systems are still research prototypes, they may run on only relatively high-end machines (Sun Workstations or even supercomputers, for example). All this would seem to mean that some of the most interesting new information technologies for higher education will be, for the foreseeable future, either inaccessible to most students or prohibitively expensive for schools or students to acquire.

Not necessarily. One way around this problem, again, exploits the Internet and the WWW. It is already possible for stand-alone software systems to piggyback on the near-standard protocols for creating WWW documents. In doing so, these systems can be made available very widely and relatively cheaply.

As anyone who uses the WWW knows, Web browsers and servers, unlike most software, run on a wide range of machines. The considerable complexities of making key languages (such as HTML) and protocols (such as HTTP) de facto standards are hidden from the average user, who can happily create documents that will appear on any machine just about the same as they look on his or hers. Technically, only WWW documents enjoy this relative machine independence. However, using scripting languages (e.g., CGI) that enable programs to be initiated on remote machines and new homepages to be created and loaded on the fly, it is possible to turn almost any piece of educational software into a distance-learning application.

The cleverness needed to turn isolated software into sharable distance-learning systems on the WWW might be of technical interest to some readers. (Certainly the exercise has fascinated the authors.) But such technical subtleties miss the key point of the example: Already, the Internet and WWW permit high-powered applications that run only on high-powered machines to be accessed by students who might have available only low-end machines – and almost any kind of low-end machine, not just those that the original application developer envisioned.

The future looks even more promising, on several scores. First, as already noted, ultra-cheap Internet appliances should bring down access cost even further. Second, the protocols needed to make products widely sharable across the Internet, using almost any hardware platform, are quickly falling into place. Tricks now required to turn the WWW into an interactive medium will soon lose their appeal, primarily because new Web tools, and languages such as Java, for building "live computational objects" (it is misleading to call them "documents" any longer), will soon provide primitives that make this kind of interactivity easy to achieve rather than a challenging problem to solve.

All this may mean that higher education can have its cake and eat it too. Most of the current cutting-edge information-technology applications we reviewed promise to help students learn better or faster, or both. Improving educational productivity in this sense is clearly an important goal for higher education. But, until recently, this goal seemed at odds with others: reducing the cost of delivering education and increasing access to education by an increasingly diverse population of students. Without question, in the future, most applications of technology in education that offer exciting possibilities for transforming teaching and learning will continue to be developed in corporate and university research settings on high-end machines. And these will probably remain expensive, well beyond the means of almost all students and even most higher-education departments and computer labs. However, high-bandwidth networks, coupled with increasingly standardized software languages and communication protocols, and with ever-cheaper Internet terminals, should bring these cutting-edge applications within reach of learners and teachers who do not have access to the newest and fastest technologies.

This does not mean that poor students will enjoy all the same access to technology-based learning as wealthy ones, of course. There will always be computers that offer more functionality at a higher price. And even if high-quality educational materials could be accessed by anyone on any machine at any time, nothing right now prevents providers from metering this access and charging whatever the market will bear. The point, however, is that information technology by itself will no longer be a significant barrier to access; if anything, the WWW and Internet should be a force toward greater access to and equity in education.

Reflection: Many Interesting Options

Certainly information technologies do more than provide better tools with which to deliver instruction and learning materials in higher education, but such tools still dominate the field of educational technology. We have discussed (or at least pointed to) a wide range of these applications, focusing especially on those that exploit the WWW, or could do so. Stepping back from the many specifics, several general points should be emphasized.

First, it should be obvious that information technologies offer many different ways to improve instruction delivery, not just one. Looking just at distance learning, there is a rich set of options to choose from. Selecting from the different choices demands attention to the (often implicit) educational goals the technologies address.

Some might help higher-education institutions reduce costs; others look better suited to increasing access to educational resources, or to increasing the quantity, quality, or speed of-student learning. Overall, the proliferation of Internet and WWW resources should steadily bring down the cost of all educational software products and services. Yet, some will be more costly than others, and a few will still be very expensive for the foreseeable future.

In general, then, it is a mistake to assume that information technology provides one or a few ways to improve learning and teaching, and it is equally wrong to believe that technology applications will affect just a single educational goal: cost reduction.

A third assumption, probably more widely believed, is also wrong: that information technology is mainly a vehicle to enhance educational productivity. Look back for a moment at the last few information-technology applications. While some, such as SHERLOCK, clearly intend to help speed up learning, or to improve learning of well-defined subject areas, it is much less obvious how others are trying to improve educational productivity in any simple sense. Instead, they are generally trying to transform the *processes* and *products* of learning. For example, they might exploit new visualization technologies to enable junior students to learn about complex systems that previously only graduate students found comprehensible; and they might foster deeper understanding through inquiry-based learning rather than traditional lectures, or through collaborative-learning methods that simply never existed prior to high-bandwidth networks.

In short, here information technology is a driver of educational reform, not of productivity enhancement — unless *productivity* is redefined to include a wide range of qualitative changes, not just quantitative improvements.

That these applications *transform* processes and products of learning more than they *enhance* productivity has several implications for their adoption, implementation, and costs. Consider, from the point of view of the developer, how many different facets of an educational context might need to change for the potentially impressive benefits of such applications to be realized. Clearly, the technology itself — the tools actually used by students in learning — is just the tip of the iceberg. Other possible changes range from the roles of teachers, to methods of evaluating learning, to deeper philosophical views of how learning happens and what constitutes knowledge.

Here is what the CoVis researchers say about their project and goals: "Traditionally, K-12 science education has consisted of the teaching of well-established facts. This approach bears little or no resemblance to the question-centered, collaborative practice of real scientists. Through the. use of advanced technologies, the Covis Project is attempting to transform science learning to better resemble the authentic practice of science.

The CoVis Project will explore issues of scaling, diversity, and sustainability as they relate to the use of networking technologies to enable high school students to work in collaboration with remote students, teachers, and scientists. An important outcome of this work will be the construction of distributed electronic communities dedicated to science learning.

Participating students study atmospheric and environmental sciences through inquiry-based activities. Using state of the art scientific visualization software, specially modified to be appropriate to a learning environment, students have access to the same research tools and data sets used by leading-edge scientists in the field.

The CoVis Project provides students with a range of collaboration and communication tools. These include: desktop video teleconferencing; shared software environments for remote, real-time collaboration; access to the resources of the Internet; a multimedia scientist's "notebook"; and scientific visualization software.

In addition to deploying new technology, we work closely with teachers at participating schools to develop new curricula and new pedagogical approaches that take advantage of project-enhanced science learning. "Collaborative Visualization" thus refers to development of scientific understanding which is mediated by scientific visualization tools in a collaborative context.

The CoVis Project seeks to understand how science education could take broad advantage of these capabilities, providing motivating experiences for students and teachers with contemporary science tools and topics.

Here are a few of the transformations in traditional classroom practice needed to realize these goals:

- *Philosophy of learning and teaching.* Learning is no longer viewed as absorbing information but constructing meaning (instructionism vs. constructionism); inquiry rather than drill-and-practice is the preferred means of acquiring knowledge; and visualization as well as text-based comprehension is a key approach to understanding.
- *Teachers' roles (and training).* Teachers act as mentors and guides to information resources, rather than as lecturers and sole sources of knowledge; they also must be fluent with new collaboration and visualization technologies.
- Students' tasks. Students learn mainly through inquiry structured by projects; most projects are done in collaboration with other students and external experts (through network connections), rather than individually.
- *Curriculum structure.* Curricula are organized around authentic projects that embed long-term tasks comparable to those tackled by professionals in the field; small-scale tasks, such as solving collection of algebra questions, are largely abandoned.
- *Classroom organization.* Classes are organized conceptually and physically by projects and computer networks. As students conduct their inquiries, the networks connect students and their tasks to external databases and experts who are sources of information, support, and commentary. Students spend little time engaged in paperwork at desks.
- *Evaluation strategies.* Authentic evaluation strategies replace traditional ones; students are evaluated on the basis of the quality of their projects, rather than their scores on short-answer or multiple-choice tests.

Figure 4-11: What It Might Take to Make CoVis Work

All of this is roughly consistent with a simple rule we have distilled from our own research in developing and implementing educational technology: If a technology fits into an existing educational process and tries to enhance existing educational products, you spend 75 percent of your time developing the technology and 25 percent worrying about all other implementation issues; if a technology tries to transform educational processes and products, you spend 75 percent of your time attending to these non technical, often complex, and frequently invisible changes in institutional practice and structure.

If anything, our 75/25 rule understates some of the complexities and costs of integrating cutting-edge applications into the classroom. True, it does suggest that deep institutional changes might be necessary to make the best use of some information technologies. However, it also seems to imply that we can anticipate the best ways to use these tools in advance, and that the biggest challenge will be to change the educational system to reflect what society knows it needs to learn and teach.

Although this statement is probably far too optimistic, who would have imagined a decade ago that visualization technologies or simulated worlds would open new educational experiences to learners? By the same token, it is extremely difficult to predict with any confidence what new and interesting applications of information technology for learning will surface over the next decade, or to imagine the kinds of institutional changes that might be necessary to best exploit these new tools.

This is not to argue that all good applications of the Internet and WWW to deliver education are shrouded in mystery. Again, there will be many options to choose from. Some applications perhaps simple Internet distance-learning tools and the next generation of ITS may continue to fit well into existing higher-education structures and to reduce costs or increase teacher productivity, others may give rise to new structures and cause us to rethink our ideas of educational productivity, and a few may transform learning in completely unexpected ways.

5

Improvement in Instruction and Learning Materials

Information technology not only provides new options for instruction delivery, it can also help create new instruction and learning materials. (What is the point of electronic delivery if there is nothing to deliver?) In turn, these new methods and tools can address some of the key challenges for higher education, including responding more nimbly to changes in demand and competing with new providers. As before, information technology provides not one or two, but several ways of improving the development of instruction and learning materials. Some options are relatively simple extensions of current methods, while others are novel.

Expanding Traditional Methods of Production

To simplify slightly, the traditional pipeline for producing educational materials (and intellectual artifacts, in general) has four key components:

- Authors create documents.
- Publishers mainly manufacture and market copies of these products.

- Libraries primarily acquire, store, and distribute copies of the products to the nearby community.
- Readers consume the products.

These groups have played relatively stable roles in the publication process for decades, even centuries. However, information technology is changing these roles; equally important, it is transforming the copyright and intellectual-property-rights laws that underpin relationships among the participants.

The simplest view of this change argues that new information technologies will reduce, perhaps even eliminate, the need for publishers and libraries. Historically, publishers and libraries have been essential intermediaries, enabling authors and audiences to reach one another. Authors rarely possessed the tools, skills, and capital necessary to typeset their books, calculate the size of production runs, or coordinate with vendors. By the same token, individual readers (especially students and researchers) rarely could afford to acquire vast libraries of literary holdings. Publishers and libraries have traditionally met these needs. However, as educational products become increasingly digital and networked, one line of argument goes, the latter two groups may prove unnecessary, at least from a technical perspective.

Today, academic research provides the most-impressive examples of how higher education is exploiting information technology to simplify the document-production pipeline. (This is hardly surprising, considering that, as we have already noted, the Internet was an active tool in scholarly research long before it played a significant role in instruction.) Members of several research communities in medicine, mathematics, and the physical sciences now publish their work, at least in "preprint" form, on the Internet. The growth of such publications has been explosive: The first electronic academic journals came online in 1991; by mid-1995, more than 300 populated cyberspace; in July 1996, according to the Association of Research Libraries, there were almost 1700 electronic journals and newsletters; and estimates ballooned to over 5000 by early 1998. Although individual publishers have been quick to add organization and decoration, many of these works, in their simplest form, comprise a collection of homepages that can be read at a distance using

Researchers have made the transition from print to bits in several steps – a process that is still continuing. In 1991 scientists at Los Alamos National Laboratory took the first step by setting up a service to distribute "e-prints" (electronic versions of paper preprints) over the Internet. Since then, their service has grown to handle over 40,000 requests per day.

The next step is to put the whole journal review and publication process online. Researchers now submit their articles by e-mail or the Web, editors send them electronically to reviewers, and the final revised versions are published in an electronic journal. As a result, turnaround time for publication is now a few weeks, not months; subscription rates are usually a fraction of those of paper journals, and sometimes free.

A third step is just now being taken. Some sites that began as single journals are adding new publications and new functionality. BioMedNet, for example, offers researchers a library of publications, search services to help locate titles, job listings, and several other kinds of assistance for professionals.

Figure 5-1: Scholar As Publisher: Making Research Directly Available to Readers Across the Internet

Provided that you know the Internet location of an online journal, accessing the current issue (if there is one; some electronic magazines simply accumulate publications over time) is simply a matter of entering the address and reading what comes up on your screen.

This kind of publication is gaining popularity for several reasons. Cutting out the traditional publisher intermediary not only dramatically speeds up the rate at which new ideas get into "print"; it also cuts publication costs and provides a direct link to readers, who can access the papers from anywhere on the Internet as soon as they are available. The audience, in turn, is often encouraged to be publishers in return, using e-mail to send feedback and reviews on articles directly back to authors. Finally, problems of calibrating production runs, disposing of unsold inventory, and dealing with unsatisfied consumer demand simply do not arise with digital, networked publications. No longer do students and faculty need to wait for other scholars to return copies of popular books: They simply print their own copies on demand.

Digital Libraries: New Media

If libraries existed only to store copies of books and other physical artifacts, and to share them with members of nearby communities, then the preceding examples might suggest that such institutions are in danger of extinction. Not surprisingly, traditional libraries are not ready to give up the ghost just yet. Along with publishers, whose traditional roles are similarly threatened, libraries are attempting to redefine their functions in ways that maintain roles for them in the delivery of information in digital, networked environments.

New digital libraries can try to go beyond being paperless versions of traditional libraries in at least three ways. First, freed of the need to store copies of documents, they can focus more on services that will help students and faculty find and organize information in vast virtual collections. Second, freed of the need to maintain collections in locations physically near their communities of readers, they can plan to aggregate virtual holdings into more encompassing, complete, and up-to-date collections. And, third, freed of the dominance of static print (audio and video can be digitized as readily as can typed text), digital libraries can grapple with the complexities of representing and cataloguing new multimedia documents.

A number of projects are engaged in the important, but painfully slow, translation of paper products into digital form. Project Gutenberg, for example, aims to have 10,000 texts online by the year 2001; with a growing network of volunteers, it is now downloading about eight new titles per month. The project's mission is to provide universal access to texts. For this reason, it is digitizing only materials in the public domain, and it is using the most basic storage format: "plain vanilla ASCII."

Already today, then, a student using almost any computer coupled to the Internet can read the complete works of Shakespeare. The National Digital Library, part of the Library of Congress, has used its considerable resources to digitize several hundred thousand Library holdings. Not limited to simple text, these holdings range from documents of the Continental Congress, to turn-of-the-century films, to Matthew Brady's Civil War photographs. Many students and scholars are even now making serious use of the Library's historical collections, reference materials, and search tools.

Tools to Find and Organize Information

As impressive as these conversion efforts are, though, even a quick scan of the burgeoning literature on digital libraries shows that most of the action is elsewhere. Few of the universities funded through the Digital Libraries Initiative, for instance, have yet to build or acquire substantial digital holdings. Rather, they are developing tools and software agents with which digital libraries can be constructed and can be effectively searched by students, faculty, and researchers.

To anyone who has browsed the WWW — which itself can be viewed as a vast and unorganized digital library — the need for these search and management tools is obvious. Most of the information available on the Internet today is of questionable quality, at best. As holdings merge, it will become more and more difficult to find high-quality products, let alone products relevant to a chosen topic. Even more problematic, traditional tools for managing this search probably will not help much in new digital libraries. Quite aside from the fact that traditional schemes barely work even today (card catalogs and huge cross-referencing tomes almost always seem to need the skills of experienced librarians), these print-indexing tools simply do not scale up well to multimedia documents that include several varieties of visual and auditory materials, as well as text. The hope is that a new generation of digital library tools and software agents will be able to

---

Subject matter/content:

The content will emphasize a diverse collection, focused on earth and space sciences, which can satisfy the needs of many different types of users. The content will be supplied by publishers, although the project will eventually allow all users to publish their work. A related project, the Journal Storage Project (JSTOR), will digitize and make available all issues from the first publication through 1990 of ten economics journals to the NSF-UMDL.

Testbed description:

The UMDL will consider a complex array of technical and socioeconomic issues and will focus the research through the design, construction, and evaluation by real users of a test bed system. The testbed will consist of a cooperating set of three types of software agents: user interface agents, mediation agents, and collection agents.

User interface agents will conduct interviews with users to establish their needs such as what they need to know, and the breadth and depth of the information they require. The interface agent will also enable the user to specify areas of interest so that the system can notify the user of items of potential relevance.

Mediation agents will coordinate searches of many distinct but net- worked collections by taking orders from the interface agents. This will allow the user to search many libraries simultaneously in ways that meet time, relevancy, and economic constraints. The mediation agents will depend upon a conspectus that describes the contents of the various collections on the network.

Collection interface agents are associated with each specific collection and can handle searching within specific collections of text, images, graphics, audio and video. Information held in the collections may be owned by various entities, some of which may demand some control over dissemination of contents or compensation for access to their copyrighted material. The system design will provide mechanisms to protect information access and support remuneration operations.

The users of the digital library testbed will include expert researchers, students, and the general public. The library will include media types ranging from page images to interactive, compound documents and eventually real-time interaction with data. Critical to the exploitation of these resources will be ongoing programs of evaluation, training, user assistance, and outreach.

Figure 5-2: Providing Services to Manage Information in Digital Libraries

Multimedia documents, and that they will be as easy to use as they are powerful. Some of these tools are little more than user-friendly search engines, which find titles through keyword searches. But others might fulfill, in electronic form, many of the roles of a personalized library assistant or online note-taker.

Aggregating Single Libraries into Mega-Libraries

Another way in which libraries are trying to grow beyond their paper counterparts is simply to merge holdings. Such aggregation rarely happens in traditional libraries: One-of-a-kind documents are closely guarded and are regarded as highly limited resources that curators are naturally reluctant to part with; the cost of moving, re-cataloguing, and repositioning artifacts usually is prohibitive; and merging libraries into a centralized location threatens to reduce access to materials by many readers in the affected communities.

Access to materials in digital libraries, by contrast, is independent of distance, so merging can only add to the resources available to communities. Moreover, merging digital holdings is comparatively trivial. Sometimes, libraries can be merged just by adding a few well placed menu items, and smart search tools can overcome many of the resulting duplications that may arise from such merging. (For example, duplicate finds, or "hits," can be automatically eliminated before search results are presented to the student.) And, if mergers are planned a little more carefully at the outset (also often aided by digital merging and interface-building tools), users can be presented an interface with the look and feel of a single digital "mega-library" rather than a collection of smaller ones, each with a different interaction protocol.

Today, even the largest digital libraries are small; while the Library of Congress houses over 100 million "traditional" artifacts, its online counterpart, the National Digital Library, "houses" a few hundred thousand, at most. When digital libraries finally acquire substantial holdings, they will have promise for addressing several important goals and problems of higher education, the first being costs. Costs could drop substantially. From a technical perspective, a document need cost no more than the price of producing it on a nearby high quality laser printer, which would easily undercut the price of common university texts, not to mention rare volumes. Of course, publishers are unlikely to tolerate such indiscriminate copying of their property, at least as copyright law now stands. However, by aggregating their acquisitions, digital college libraries are already discovering that they can use their coordinated buying power to negotiate much more effective licensing deals than publishers are willing to offer on books.

Digital libraries can improve access to educational material even as they reduce access cost, thereby promising to be a key component in future distance-learning curricula. Students within a university will enjoy better access to digital materials, in part because they will be able to use them at any place and any time, not just in library study halls; and they will not have to wait for days or weeks until popular titles are returned to the shelf. More interestingly, as digital libraries merge, students can access the very best materials, regardless of their institutional affiliation.

Even if such mergers do not happen officially, students may be able to implement them informally. Today, for example, nothing prevents University of Michigan students on the Web from accessing.

Librarians, Unite — For Buying Power

College librarians are banding together to purchase electronic resources for their institutions. "We've found that this sort of grouppurchasing power has really enabled us to leverage the dollars that we have and to get resources we couldn't have otherwise," says an associate librarian at the University of Texas at Austin, which buys publications through the TexShare consortium. The group buying arrangement is also advantageous for publishers, who don't need to spend as much on marketing: "As a group, we'll pay the vendor more money than they can realistically get by slogging it out school by school," says the executive director of OhioLINK, which includes more than 40 colleges and universities. The president of Britannica Online figures that more than half of the 293 institutions using his product are doing so under consortium-based licenses.

Figure 5-3: Bigger Is Better?

Digital holdings at Stanford, MIT, University of Illinois, or any of the other dozens of online libraries. For that matter, nothing prevents any Internet user — say, an unemployed worker in Detroit or a teenager in Harlem — from perusing these digital documents.

This may not be true for long, however. It is quite easy for universities to put up "firewalls," which permit access only to their students and faculty. Technically easy, yes, but perhaps hard to justify; digital-library resources, unlike books, are simply not "consumed" when used. With well-designed library servers and ample bandwidth, the hundreds of authorized users of a digital library should not notice a thousand or more unofficial users.

All of this would suggest that the best world of all would be one with a single digital library, located at a single site (or perhaps distributed throughout cyberspace), and surrounded by a collection of smart, user-friendly, library tools and software agents to help find digital resources, piece them together into new documents, and share them among students and faculty. If bigger is better, why stop at merging just a few digital collections?

Obstacles to Building Productive Digital Libraries

For several reasons, this vision of the future is a long way off, even if it is a good one. To begin with, different universities and different communities may simply want to retain different digital documents; local decency laws, as well as informal cultural preferences, will continue to encourage diversity, and sometimes insularity, in digital holdings. Even discounting regional preferences, some important technical hurdles still need to be overcome.

A completely universal digital library presupposes standards for representing the different kinds of multimedia information that make up the digital documents. The de facto standards for WWW homepages (namely, HTML and HTTP) are a good first step in this direction, but they are a long way from being complete. Indeed, closure may be a receding goal, because new data formats and media types are being spawned faster than standards for existing ones are being settled. It is also important to remember that few of the artifacts now in traditional libraries (so-called legacy materials) have been digitized; they must be included in any digital library that even pretends to supplant a paper-based one. On top of all this, digital materials, no less than paper products, are subject to decay and deterioration.

Although the technical problems are substantial, perhaps the biggest obstacles to building digital libraries are legal and institutional. Higher-education institutions have a long history of independence in the way they provide services. Even if economic and social arguments point toward merging digital libraries, whether universities will enthusiastically embrace changes that might threaten their institutional identity is not clear – especially if they can convince themselves that sharing their knowledge base will lose students, and thus revenue, to competing schools.

Finally, copyright problems could kill the development of digital libraries in their infancy. Over decades, copyright law has forged a delicate balance between the interests of publishers and those of consumers, with libraries in the middle. First-sale doctrine permits libraries to lend books without requiring libraries or readers to further compensate publishers and authors. Similarly, over time, libraries have negotiated extensions of fair-use laws that allow students and faculty to (photo) copy materials without violating copyright. Current copyright law is not particularly generous to consumers, and a direct application of it to digital documents, if possible at all, would certainly not give readers the more-or-less free and unlimited copying privileges that are tacitly assumed in the scenarios we just sketched.

But even these rules would be preferable to some of the revisions of copyright now being drafted with digital materials in mind. The 1994 "Green Paper" put out by the Clinton administration's Intellectual Property Working Group, for example, would require readers to pay by use: Each time a copyrighted digital document was copied – including (the publishers hope) copies cached on a local machine whenever a document is browsed on the Web – publishers would be compensated. If these kinds of changes are enacted, students and faculty will be required to pay each time they skim virtual shelves that hold recent issues of digital periodicals. Far from looking like progress, this future could be a big step backward in public access to knowledge: How many university libraries charge admission to their reading rooms? Cyberspace-savvy academics fear, with good reason, that digital libraries will never thrive if copyright law is rewritten to be balanced so heavily in favor of publishers.

Higher Ed Groups Eye Electronic Copyright Bill

Representatives from higher education associations testified lastweek before a House subcommittee, urging lawmakers not to pass new electronic copyright rules before their impact on colleges and universities can be assessed. At issue is a revised definition of"fair use" of copyrighted digital materials that threatens toeliminate or severely restrict online interlibrary loans, and wouldalso prevent professors from using such materials as part of their courses.

Figure 5-4: Higher Education's Fight with New Electronic Copyright Laws

Digital Publishers

Publishers, of course, see the threat very differently. To them, the Internet calls up their ultimate nightmare: The U.S. Library of Congress buys one copy of a digital text for its collection, makes the copy available on interlibrary loan to any other library or patron (just as libraries generally do today), whereupon, since bits are so easily reproduced, every reader can manufacture his or her own copy with a few mouse clicks. In this scenario, the first sale of a digital book might well be the last. While admittedly fanciful, this extreme example holds more than a grain of truth. Copyright law can afford to be more generous when built-in barriers – the machinery needed to reproduce tapes, the time and cost of photocopy paper, for instance – provide natural disincentives to duplication. But these disincentives are largely gone with digital products. So, today, most publishers spend as much time defending themselves against the Internet as they do creating products for it.

Book Publishers Worry Over Threat of Internet

Publishers may not be feeling panic, but they are clearly edgy about the prospects of new technology, which many consider as potentially significant as Gutenberg's development of moveable type.

Their chief concern is the improvement of computer technology that will make it easier and faster to scan books.

In statements to the House Subcommittee on Courts and Intellectual Property Rights, the Association of American Publishers fretted about a new world: "although not wanting to be melodramatic, publishers do fear for their future, and the well-being of their authors, when looking at a world with low-cost, easy-to-use ubiquitous scanners, copiers and binders."

The publishers group commissioned several studies on the issue,including one that concluded that there is no practical way to"unilaterally prevent" unauthorized distribution of books.

Instead the association is pressing for methods to detect copyright violations with a "uniform file identifier system."

It is essentially a license plate on copyrighted work that contains the publisher's name and the identity of the person who purchased the work. The publishing industry is backing legislation before the House and Senate to make it a criminal and civil offense to alter these cyber license plates. Even they are not quite sure what form the identifying codes will take, but they do know they want them.

Figure 5-5: Who Wins: Publishers, Readers, Both, or Neither?

Over the past few years, this fear has slowly started to transform through a variety of other emotions and actions: uncertain acceptance, careful study, strategic mergers, and hasty exits. Still, recognizing a booming educational software market whose retail sales may have climbed as much as 50 percent in 1995 (to over $500 million), traditional publishing houses, together with some fresh competitors, are beginning to sell substantial quantities of new products to higher education.

Publishers Warily Eye The Net

Members of the Association of American Publishers have decided that they must become actively involved in the deployment of online information distribution systems, or get left behind in the dust. Up until now, worries over rampant unauthorized dissemination have resulted in "significant hesitation about investing" in electronic publishing, says the chairman of the AAP's Enabling Technologies Committee. Now, they've decided to try to resolve copyright issues "before copyright infringement on the network becomes very widespread and assumed to be the way the network works. It's a recognition that whereas in the past, publishing members of the AAP have been able to leave technological concerns to suppliers – such as compositors, typesetters and printers – in network publishing we cannot leave it to others."

College Textbooks – Past History?

Publishing CEOs to Address the Future of College Textbooks at ConTEXT'96. With the increasing presence of distance learning programs, custom-made course packs, and multimedia tools in higher education, the future form of learning materials remains a big question. To address some of these issues, chief executives from three publishing companies will share their insights and ideas on the future direction of the textbook publishing industry during ConTEXT '96: A Conference on Textbooks and Technology.

Learning Company Prefers Broderbund to Softkey

The Learning Company has accepted a new merger offer from Broderbund, rejecting a rival offer from Softkey, the Cambridge, Mass.-based company that has little regard for the Learning Company's management. A top Broderbund executive says, "We believe that the management of the Learning Company is one of its key assets. We're looking at a merger with a successful company that is doing a lot of things right. The last thing we want to do is alter that chemistry."

Murdoch Sells Educational Publishing Group

Rupert Murdoch's News Corporation is selling HarperCollins Publishing to the U.K.-based media conglomerate Pearson PLC. A Smith Barney analyst says that "Educational publishing doesn't fit News Corp.'s image as a global distributor of information. Rupert has a lot of different objectives, and this is not one of them." Pearson PLC will now rank fourth in educational book publishing, behind McGraw Hill, Macmillan, and Harcourt-Brace.

Figure 5-6: Traditional Publishers and the Digital Enemy: Fight or Flight?

Conservatism, however, still seems the order of the day, in at least two senses. First, the initial reaction of many large publishers has been to simply follow the lead of the pioneering academics, who are abandoning paper journals in favor of just-in-time electronic versions, following the "if you can't beat them, buy them" strategy: Some small and informal online publishing sites are being acquired by professional publishers. BioMedNet, for example, initially the brain-child of a few researchers, was taken over by Current Science, a small but fast-moving new publishing firm that specializes in value-added electronic products. Second, while publishers certainly will develop more and better digital products for higher education – BioMedNet has grown from a single digital journal to a rich, online community, for example – the processes by which new titles are created in the future probably will not be much different from what they are now.

To find places where information technology is changing the ways in which learning materials are created in a big way, we must look at a much smaller scale: the individual publisher.

Mcgraw-Hill Plans Electronic Academic Publishing

McGraw-Hill, the publishing and information services company, is considering the development of electronic academic journals that could be published more quickly and economically than traditional academic journals. An enthusiast about information technology, McGraw-Hill chairman Joseph Dionne says: "If you take this technology, you have someone submit his research, have it reviewed by knowledgeable people, the process could be done in a week or two weeks." He says he has approached such groups as the Society of Physics and the Society of Chemistry, and "there is a very real possibility that it is going to happen over the next five years."

Figure 5-7: Paper Publishing Elephants Following Digital Mice?

Internet Impact: Innovative Ways to Create New Instruction and Learning Materials

We discussed that how specific courses here might be part of a new generation of distance-learning class materials. But we look now at the Hall itself, rather than at its constituent products, to see how new instruction and learning materials are created.

The most prominent feature of the Hall is a large table that organizes specific courseware by subject matter. It is much like a standard university course catalog, except that the offerings are full sets of course materials, rather than brief course descriptions. The Hall also provides tools that allow new courses to be easily searched and added, and a "What's New" link to identify the latest entries (a very valuable resource for frequent browsers, since hundreds of courses already reside at the Hall).

The World Lecture Hall demonstrates two very powerful benefits of information technology for education – one already widely touted, the other less so. Relatively familiar is the idea that new technologies encourage individual, home-grown production. In higher education, we have seen such production in electronic journals that bypass traditional publication bottlenecks, as well as in online courses constructed by individual faculty almost from scratch, using digital materials. Outside education, the examples are often even more compelling. Today, for example, audio and video desktop publishing puts at one's fingertips the facilities that just a few years ago were available only to large, well-funded professional studios. Using these tools, small grassroots print-journalists, moviemakers, and record producers are already making significant inroads into markets traditionally dominated by big players. There is no reason to believe that, at least on technical grounds, educational publication and the creation of instructional materials will be immune to these sea changes.

The second feature has more to do with the World Lecture Hall itself, and the cooperative curriculum development it can encourage, than with the nature and origins of its constituent online courses. The Hall attempts to provide a location and supporting tools that will encourage faculty not only to create new online course materials, but to

The World Lecture Hall is a Web site managed out the University to Texas. Its main feature is a large table that organizes several hundred courses, alphabetically, by subject name. Users select a subject link, which then leads to a page listing all specific courses of that type. These course links, in turn, can be followed down to their component pieces: lecture notes, tests, and so on.

The World Lecture Hall encourages new course submissions, which may be completely original or modifications of courses already resident. However, as of 4/97, it provides relatively few tools for users or developers beyond a "What's New" link that lists recent additions, a simple search facility, and the table of course offerings itself. The Hall's developers apparently do not review courses offered by developers, follow other policies for quality control, or provide tools to help consumers find and compare products.

Figure 5-8: The World Lecture Hall

Using simple but very powerful digital cut-and-paste tools, this copy can be edited into a new course – possibly for a slightly different topic and audience, and, perhaps also a better product. In any case, the new version can be returned to the World Lecture Hall, adding to the materials available to share with the academic community. Eventually, this kind of chaotic cooperation might lead to a vast collection of digital courses of progressively better quality, as a new set of course creators stands on the shoulders of the current creators.

Challenges to Building Productive Individual Publishing Communities in Higher Education

How likely is this rosy future? On the one hand, early indications seem promising. It was quite possible that when the World Lecture Hall was established (in 1994), no one would have come to the site. At its inception, the Hall contained very few online courses, and so had little value to browsers. But, by late 1996, the Hall contained several hundred courses; according to its managers, dozens of offerings flow in each month, and the pace is increasing. In short, at least this communal repository of digital instructional material demonstrates what economists refer to as positive "network externalities": the more users adopt the product, the more valuable (but not more scarce) the product becomes for other users.

On the other hand, most home-grown products – whether in the form of videotapes, audio recordings, or Web homepages – suffer from a common problem: Although their creators view them as priceless, few others may. Just as once we were bored to tears by our neighbors' vacation slide shows, today most Web surfers are frustrated by the thousands (now probably millions) of homepages that serve only to hide the few gems they seek. In the case of virtual collections such as the World Lecture Hall, it is likely that if potential consumers (who may also be producers) cannot find quality digital course materials, they will cease browsing this site (and adding to it). If so, the number of new entries will decrease, and, with fewer shoulders to stand on, the overall quality of offerings is unlikely to improve quickly, if at all. In this future, the World Lecture Hall, far from flourishing, would probably disappear within a few semesters.

Whether or not such sites foster a productive community of grassroots publishing in higher education will depend on a number of factors. Luck and good timing may play a role. If, for example, homegrown sites develop strong early products, they may attract the attention and new contributors needed to sustain them through their formative period. Also, even if quality products exist, they must be easy to find. Internet search engines and smart agents already help consumers locate useful sites and ignore irrelevant ones. Providers also have several means at their disposal to simplify search and improve product quality. Passive tools, such as the World Lecture Hall's table organization and "What's New" option, help make navigation easier for consumers.

Other providers (although not the World Lecture Hall) take more active steps, preferring to control the quality of products they include in their collections, rather than just relying on consumers to cut through irrelevant materials with search tools. One ingenious, simple idea that virtual Yellow Pages (BigBook, for example, at www.bigbook.com/) are trying is to rely on consumer popularity to organize products and shape the market by letting users rate any business in their database and permit new buyers to see these reviews. Although this strategy has not been applied to educational courseware databases, the implementation would probably be very simple; however, the long-term consequences of using such a quality-management scheme would certainly be far from easy to predict.

Taking a more traditional approach, electronic journals such as BioMedNet have instituted formal peer-review procedures. Similarly, many of the electronic discussion groups on Usenet (the newsgroup side of the Internet) are moderated, rather than uncontrolled. Moderators can play a wide range of roles: reorganizing and packaging submitted materials, editing copy, adding commentary, and even censoring contributions outright. All this sounds very much like the value-added functions of traditional publishers. It hardly comes as a surprise, therefore, that publishing firms, seeking to redefine their roles in the digital age, are now seeking partnerships with developers of home-grown online course materials for higher education. In addition to ensuring quality and packaging of new products, many publishers are planning also to market the courseware, secure copyright agreements, and arrange licensing.

University Online

University Online, a small Internet publisher that licenses 200 ready- made high school and college courses, is working with George Washington and George Mason Universities to create tutorials and more online courses at the higher education level, and is seeking more universities for similar alliances. The company's president is working with textbook publishers to obtain the electronic rights to their materials, and will then pay the publishers' royalties and split the tuition with the universities that license its products.

Figure 5-9: Grassroots Developers and Traditional Publishers

Individual publishing on the Internet is so new that it is difficult to determine how significantly it will contribute to the creation of new instruction and learning materials. If it flourishes, however, this innovative approach could speak to several important goals and problems of higher education, such as the need for just-in-time and on demand learning.

Home-grown publishing is now technically feasible because information technologies greatly simplify constructing, editing, and sharing of documents, which may invite the creation of many low quality products. But, suitably channeled, high-volume and high speed production also has its good side. Obviously, the easier it is for individual faculty members to create courseware (or to tailor existing materials into new packages), the more they will be able to offer diverse materials to an expanding and increasingly divergent student population. Responding to a nearly overwhelming need for remedial instruction, for example, faculty from the California State University system might be able to put together a fresh physics curriculum in short order by combining some of the simpler digital simulations, assignments, and exams from any of the more than 25 physics courses now online in the World Lecture Hall.

This same flexibility could permit institutions to build new courseware and learning products that respond to the rapidly changing demands of industry – not, assuming popular predictions are right, a one-time effort. Former Labor Secretary Robert Reich, among others, claims that workers will need to retool for up to five job changes per career. If so, rapid changes in instructional materials will be the rule for the foreseeable future; and the versatility that new information technologies bring to educational production will be critical for meeting these demands.

In short, just as information technology already helps manufacturing and services industries to dramatically shorten production cycles and to help solve the challenge of just-in-time academic publishing, it could enable higher education to meet the demand for just-in-time or on-demand learning.

Reflection: Many Interesting Options, Many Hard Choices — A Reprise

Viewed broadly, information technologies might change the ways instruction and learning materials are created much as they could alter the ways instruction and learning are delivered: by providing many different kinds of applications, not just one or a few. The applications could speak to a variety of goals and problems in higher education, helping to reduce costs, enrich and diversify course offerings, expand access, and increase responsiveness to industry demands and social needs; and some of the most valuable uses of information technology will not simply improve educational productivity, but will require institutions to consider moderate or extensive structural transformations.

For example, by digitizing library holdings, universities can expect to save space, reduce acquisition costs, seamlessly combine multimedia documents with traditional text, and provide students and faculty with a new generation of tools for finding information and organizing it into intellectual products. However, although a single university can benefit from digitization, cross-institutional cooperation may be critical if digital libraries are to make the best-quality materials available to students and to reach the broadest audience. As we have noted, copyright problems will challenge this kind of library merging, as will barriers between higher-education institutions.

By the same token, smaller, grassroots publishers on the Web, rather than larger, traditional publishing firms, look to be nimbler providers of new digital courseware that will meet changing industry needs. But, at least today, the individual publication process is chaotic, to say the least. In the World Lecture Hall, for instance, faculty often cut and paste new curricula from previous offerings, with little concern for copyright or institutional origin. This kind of highly informal cross-institutional collaboration has been common in academic research. Nevertheless, in the past, most higher-education institutions have been much more reluctant to share their course offerings, informally or otherwise. So, as with digital libraries, individual academic publishing may stress or even transform existing institutional structures, rather than simply enabling them to operate more productively without fundamental change.

A slightly different way to view all this is that the Internet is beginning to foster new academic and learning communities across the Web, most of which are organizing along functional lines: developing courseware, conducting research, sharing curricula, for instance. Common interests and expertise are much more important in defining these communities than is distance, an impediment that cheap, high-bandwidth connectivity largely erases. For similar reasons, most cyberspace communities tend to ignore institutional boundaries when those boundaries interfere with emerging functional interests. These forces are beginning to give rise to new communities of practice that, at the very least, crisscross previous structures and may even erode old higher-education structures while building new ones.

6

World Wide Web as a Teaching Resource

History and Context

The first computer was connected to the Internet in 1969, and in subsequent decades, computer networks grew slowly around the world. In the United Kingdom (UK), computer networks for academic use are now provided by the United Kingdom Educational and Research Networking Association (UKERNA), which operates, among other things, the Joint Academic Network (JANET). JANET is funded by "top-slicing" the government funding for education so that individual institutions do not have to pay for network connectivity, except to the extent that their government funding for other purposes is reduced. When JANET was first set up in the 1980s, it used its own set of protocols related to the ISO/CCITT protocols. By the early 1990s, however, it became obvious that the use of Internet protocols would soon be universal, and JANET was switched to Internet protocols. By 1995, an increasing number of local colleges and schools were connected to JANET and using Internet protocols. JANET is connected to other U. K. Internet access providers via the London Internet Exchange, but UKERNA provides links to North America and Europe exclusively for the use of institutions connected to JANET.

Wolverhampton is an industrial town of about 250,000 people in the center of England, on the western edge of the West Midlands industrial conurbation. The University of Wolverhampton was founded as Wolverhampton Technical College in 1932 and has gradually expanded since becoming a polytechnic (a degree-issuing institution without the title of University) in 1969 and a university in 1992. Its first computer science degree course ran in 1967, when the main equipment consisted of an ancient relay computer built by the U. K. Atomic Energy Research establishment in 1948 and donated in 1957. This machine, which can still be seen in Birmingham Science Museum, had 90 memory locations and took 2 seconds to add up two numbers. The present equipment consists of well over 2,000 personal computers mostly in general purpose, open-access laboratories, along with various Sun servers and specialist workstations.

In 1984, the Polytechnic acquired its first off-site computer network connection using the U. K. PSS service for E-mail only, on a dial-up basis. In 1988, a permanent 9600 baud JANET connection was obtained, which used JANET's own protocols. In October 1992, the connection was upgraded to a 64 kbaud line using ISDN and Internet protocols. The connection was quickly saturated, and in July 1995 it was upgraded to 4 Mbaud. The university provides several (currently about 20) dial-up lines for student use running at a maximum of 33.6 kbaud. All computers are networked and Internet enabled.

Readers outside the U. K. should know that at the time of writing, a typical high performance personal computer cost approximately Rs 25,000, about 2 to 3% of the average professional salary. Telephone calls were charged by the minute; a local call typically cost about Rs0.60 per minute (off peak). A number of the university's modems are connected to the telephone system operated by the local cable television company, and calls to these modems are free (off peak) to customers who also buy a cable television package. This package is very popular with students.

Use of the Internet for Teaching

In the University of Wolverhampton's School of Computing, several lecturers have for some time been interested in using the

Internet to support teaching activities. We have particularly concentrated on a course called Social, Legal and Professional Aspects of Computing known as SLAPA throughout this paper. This course contributes 12.5% of the credits for the final year of the computer science degree programs; it is also included in various postgraduate and foreign exchange programs. The course has been a good choice to study the use of the Internet: The students have a wide range of computer backgrounds and skills. The SLAPA course has used the ubiquitous public domain Internet tools, anonymous file transfer protocol (FTP), Gopher, and most recently the World Wide Web (WWW) to deliver resources and pointers to students.

Anonymous FTP

FTP is the Internet mechanism for transferring files from one computer to another. People normally require a log-in account on the remote computer before transferring a file from it, but the many Unix systems have a special user account known as anonymous which does not require a password and thus allows anybody to access files. This process effectively allows people to publish material via the Internet by placing it in the anonymous file area.

As soon as the university was connected to the Internet, we discovered that many files were available at no cost from any one of a significant number of anonymous FTP servers. We also discovered that several Archie servers maintained searchable indexes to the material available on the various anonymous FTP servers across the Internet. For our computer scientists, this was a bonanza, but much of the material was computer science related, and anonymous FTP sites seemed to offer little to support general educational needs.

This lack of support was partly due to the difficulty of identifying resources by file name (Archie servers identify only file names), particularly when the resources are subject to the MS-DOS 8 + 3 constraint, and partly due to the unfamiliarity with the Internet among university staff. The computer scientists persisted and helped by the discovery of a spare disk drive, constructed the university's own anonymous FTP archive, which serves material to a few specialist courses such as Business Data Communications and makes staff authored material publicly available. The creation of an anonymous FTP archive is not difficult, particularly for those familiar with Unix, but the standard software available had deficiencies that we had to correct ourselves.

Here is an extract from the results of an Archie search for privacy:

Host rzbsdi01.uni-trier.de

Location: /pub/info/faq DIRECTORY drwxr-xr-x 512 Mar 20 1996 alt.privacy DIRECTORY drwxr-xr-x 512 Feb 18 1996 comp.society.privacy

Host ftp.seas.gwu.edu

Location: /pub/rtfm/alt DIRECTORY drwxr-xr-x 512 Sep 27 04:08 privacy

Host ftp.rice.edu

Location: /tmp_mnt/ftp/ftp/net/cwis/cwis/gopher/world/Policies/.old/Owlnet/.cap FILE -rw-r—r— 46 Jan 1 1970 privacy

Location: /tmp_mnt/ftp/ftp/net/cwis/cwis/gopher/world/Policies/.old/Owlnet FILE -rw-r—r—162 Jan 1 1970 privacy

Host ftp.cs.uchicago.edu

Location: /pub/discussions/hypernews/cpsr FILE -rw-rw-r— 456 Aug 11 1995 privacy

As can be seen, apart from the file names, this extract gives little clue to the nature and format of the information; teachers intending to locate resources in this way must spend a considerable amount of time and effort downloading and reviewing resources to determine their suitability.

Gopher

Gopher is a menu-driven system of linked Internet resources. It enjoyed considerable popularity in the early 1990s before the general acceptance of the WWW. In 1994, we decided to use Gopher to deliver resources related to computer privacy to students studying the SLAPA course. Once a student had started the Gopher application, he or she was greeted with a menu looking like this Internet Gopher Information Client v2.0.16.

The cursor key can be used to move the pointer up and down, and the Return key to select a particular item. All the items shown here had been found on the Internet by various means and were copied to our local Gopher server. The descriptive text shown on the previous menu corresponds to the file names on the server. It was also necessary to create a Capability directory entry.

Creating the necessary files in the Gopher hierarchy was not totally straightforward; it required some system knowledge. If we had persevered with this approach, it would doubtless have become simpler. The students seemed happy with this way of providing information, and regarded it as a significant improvement on using Archie and anonymous FTP archives. The main disadvantage was the fact that these were local copies of text files and did not contain pointers to any further resources; thus teachers were responsible for selecting suitable files. The practice of making local copies is also questionable in the context of intellectual property rights, but our slow link to the Internet at the time forced us to take this approach.

Although Gopher has now been eclipsed by the WWW we still find it a useful means of navigating the large number of text and other files in our anonymous FTP archive, particularly for users accessing the archive via the WWW. We intend to keep the Gopher server operational for this purpose.

The World Wide Web

The development of the WWW started in 1990, but it was not used at the university until late 1993, and the first server was not set up until mid-1994. It quickly became apparent that the WWW was an effective way to distribute attractive, prepared material to a wide audience. The ability to include links to other resources made creating a list of resources for students simple, once a teacher had identified the resources.

The SLAPA module was one of the first to adopt this approach. The WWW was used to make lists of resources available to students, and students were also required to prepare Web pages on selected topics as part of the coursework assessment of the module. As we have reported elsewhere, this successful although comparatively slow access to some resources resulted in some unfavorable comparisons to resources delivered via conventional library methods and via CD-ROMs. It was pleasing to note that students were happy to prepare and present the results of their own work as Web pages.

The university's Internet link was upgraded from 64 kBaud to 4 MBaud in 1995. The increased speed and responsiveness, coupled with a rapidly increasing general awareness of the Internet and the WWW, resulted in an increased readiness to use the WWW for distributing teaching material. It was decided to conduct a much more extensive survey of Internet usage among SLAPA students. The results are presented here.

SLAPA Survey Results

These results come from a survey of student attitudes to electronic dissemination and gathering of information. The survey was conducted by questionnaire in May 1996. Eighty-three replies were received from students studying SLAPA. As part of their assessment, students were required to research topics such as on-line shopping and intellectual property issues associated with the Internet and to prepare presentations based on the results of their researches both orally and in the form of Web pages. The students taking the module were comprised of three groups: a group of 66 students who were nearly all final-year undergraduates; a group of 11 students who were finishing a 1-year postgraduate (MSc) conversion course; a group of 6 German exchange students from various courses. Most questions on the questionnaire were to be answered by circling a number in the range of 1 to 5. The suggested answers had a value or weight from most positive to most negative, which enabled weighted results to be calculated. The weights for the individual responses and the weighted totals are shown in the following tables. There was some evidence that some of the German students misunderstood the instructions, and the results for this group should be treated with caution. Not all students answered all questions, and so the numbers do not always add up.

The first set of questions asked about using the WWW to complete assignments.

The weighted totals for the other groups were 3.30, 3.30, and 3.33 for the postgraduate conversion-course students and 3.17, 3.17, and 2.82 for the German students. These figures suggest that both groups were less happy with information technology than were the final-year undergraduates, a conclusion supported by many of the following results; the postgraduate and German student groups were much smaller, however.

TABLE 6-1: Results: Use of WWW to Complete Assignments

Statement	*Agree Strongly*	*Agree*	*No Strong Opinion or Don't Know*	*Disagree*	*Disagree Strongly*	*Weighted*
	(1)	*(2)*	*(3)*	*(4)*	*(5)*	*Total*
The information you found was useful.	17	28	14	6	1	2.18
The information was easy to find.	10	31	11	11	2	2.45
It was easy to print.	9	20	14	11	8	2.82

TABLE 6-2: Results: Questions About Library and CD-ROM

	Had you used thefollowing previously?						*Which would you prefer to use?*		
Group	Library		CD-ROM		WWW		Library	CD-ROM	WWW
	Yes	No	Yes	No	Yes	No			
Under-graduate	58	7	54	11	56	12	11	10	42
Post-graduate	9	1	8	2	5	5	4	1	4
German	5	1	4	2	5	1	0	1	5

The two questions shown in Table 6.2 asked about previous experience using the library and CD-ROMs. A question on previous experience using the WWW was asked later in a separate part of the survey. The results have been included here for comparison purposes. Students were also asked which medium they preferred. The most striking figure in this set of results is the high preference shown for the use of the WWW to discover information. This finding is in conspicuous contrast to our earlier researches that had shown some preference for CD-ROMs; we concluded that these results were based on perceptions that the WWW was rather slow compared to CD-ROMs.

Questionnaire respondents were also asked whether they had any comments about the various media. Some of the comments are worth quoting. "WWW can be used from more locations": This response related to the fact that using conventional library resources clearly requires a physical trip to the library, and similar constraints apply to the use of CD-ROMs. CD-ROM equipped personal computers are still uncommon at the university, and the university's stock of CD-ROMs is based in the library. Further, we do not have any networked CD-ROM drives so after a student has borrowed a CD-ROM, it is unavailable to anybody else until it is returned. It is likely that the falling price of CD-ROM-equipped computers will make them more common, but a library of CD-ROMs poses similar problems to a library of books. In contrast, the WWW is accessible from any of the university's computers, all of which are Internet connected, support some flavor of MS-Windows , and have either Netscape (Netscape Communications Corporation;) or Mosaic (National Center for Supercomputing Applications, University of Illinois at Urbana-Champaign; WWW browsers as part of their standard software. Students with home computers can also access the WWW conveniently. The technology for multiple users to access a single CD-ROM does seem to be under active development.

"WWW is more likely to be up-to-date": This response might be more of a perception than a fact. At the time of the survey , the WWW was still a rather new medium, and practically everything available on the WWW would have been created in the 2 previous years. Whether this will continue to be the case remains to be seen; informal discussions with various colleagues have highlighted the WWW's impermanence as a potential problem for its long-term use.

"WWW is often slow at peak times": This problem is familiar to all Internet users and is well discussed in the literature. Proposals and hints of proposals that future Internet users would have to pay more for reliable high-speed access are worrying to educators. Our particular context has several features that make this problem worse. For the SLAPA course, many identified resources were located in North America, hardly surprising as we share a common language. The transatlantic Internet links available to the U. K. academic community, however, are not particularly fast and are often congested. Further, in early mornings U. K. time, access is noticeably fast until American users start work, when things start getting much slower and stay that way until about midnight U. K. time. Unfortunately, very few students choose to do their work during the faster access times.

TABLE 6-3: Results: Constructing and Using Web Pages

Statement	*Agree strongly*	*Agree*	*No Strong Opinion or Don't Know*	*Dis-agree*	*Dis-agree Strongly*	*Weighted Total*
	(1)	*(2)*	*(3)*	*(4)*	*(5)*	
Web pages were easy to construct.	17	28	12	7	1	2.18
Web pages were easy to put on the system	18	18	14	12	1	2.37
The instructions Supplied on the university's home pages were easy to follow.	9	25	14	5	2	2.38
I prefer producing a Web page to doing an oral presentation.	25	24	8	4	5	2.09
I prefer producing a Web page to writing an essay or report.	17	14	16	10	4	2.51
I learned more looking at other Students' Web pages than from listening to their presentations.	4	15	25	12	1	2.84

"WWW has more information than CD-ROM": This response was rather interesting. The students were given a set of links to identified resources, and they then followed the hyperlinks or in several cases went directly to the search engines. Any attempt to estimate the size of the WWW seems futile, but at the time of writing, the larger search engines claimed to have indexed over 60 million pages with an average size of about 6 kilobytes, a total of 360 gigabytes of information. This is about 500 times the 600-megabyte maximum information on a CD-ROM, but many CD-ROMs include a much higher proportion of multimedia content than does the WWW. It is clearly unrealistic to expect a library of CD-ROMs to contain the same amount of information, yet questions about information duplication and information quality must concern teachers.

The weighted totals for the other groups were 3.12, 3.62, 3.86, 2.75, 3.00, and 3.40 for the postgraduates and 3.00, 3.40, 3.00, 3.00, 3.33, and 3.00 for the German students. The most notable figures here are related to the difficulty encountered in creating and installing pages. The undergraduate group found this a fairly straightforward task, and thus these findings confirmed earlier results, but the postgraduates, with comparatively little experience, found it much more difficult (3.62 versus 2.37). The differences most probably arose because installing pages on "the system" required some knowledge of the Unix environment to which the postgraduates, who had only otherwise encountered MS-Windows-based software, were rather hostile.

The next three sets of questions were concerned with general information technology issues. The first set of questions dealt with attitudes to and use of Email. The weighted results for the other groups of students were 2.20, 2.55, 2.44, 2.44, and 3.38 for the postgraduates and 2.33, 1.40, 2.20, 2.20, and 4.00 for the German students. Several respondents expressed concern that assignments submitted by E-mail could go astray. It has certainly been our experience that misaddressed or misfiled e-mail is more difficult to recover than is paper that has gone astray, and any teacher contemplating receipt of assessments via E-mail should encourage students to keep backup copies on disk. The host operating system date stamps on such files should provide proof that the work was done before the handling date.

The next set of questions concerned the use of bulletin boards and the Usenet. The weighted totals for the other groups were 2.90, 2.60, 2.89, 3.11, 3.40, and 3.11 for the postgraduate students and 2.67, 2.33, 3.00, 2.33, 4.50, and 4.50 for the German students.

Although a local Usenet newsgroup had been created as a forum for discussion of issues related to the SLAPA course, nobody posted anything to it. The reason is not clear although lack of publicity may well have been significant.

TABLE 6.4: Questions About Attitudes to E-mail

Statement	*Agree strongly*	*Agree*	*No Strong Opinion or Don't Know*	*Dis-agree*	*Dis-agree Strongly*	*Weighted Total*
	(1)	*(2)*	*(3)*	*(4)*	*(5)*	
I regularly read my E-mail.	41	13	1	4	6	1.78
I regularly use mail to send messages to lecturers.	22	14	14	12	3	2.38
Not all lecturers read their E-mail regulalry.	11	18	25	5	3	2.53
E-mail is impersonal	4	11	18	24	7	3.30
I think submitting assignments by E-mail is a good idea.	9	13	15	16	10	3.08

The next set of questions concerned general attitudes to and frequency of use of a variety of Internet-related tools and facilities. The weighted totals for the other groups were 4.00, 2.00, 2.56, 1.89, 1.78, 1.38, 1.78, 2.11, 3.44, and 3.22 for the postgraduate students and 3.83, 4.17, 3.17, 3.00, 2.00, 2.00, 2.83, 2.00, 4.00, and 3.83 for the German students. The results shown here clearly indicate the extent to which the WWW has already displaced earlier Internet resource discovery and access tools such as anonymous FTP and Gopher in the students' perception of how to use the Internet. This cohort of students had not encountered the use of the Internet in any other courses; later cohorts, however, will have encountered the Internet in a course called Business Data Communications, in which they are required to send each other E-mail and also to use the WWW to discover resources relevant to the course.

The Way Forward — Resources

Our experiences have suggested that students like to use the Internet and more especially, the WWW. Individual teachers and the educational community must however address several significant problems before the Internet's potential to enhance the educational experience can be fully unlocked. It is far from clear that unrestricted exposure to the multiplicity of resources available is an effective and efficient use of student time. Most teachers think that it is not, and we have often found that a number of students have wandered off into some odd corners of the WWW. There seems to be no way to stop this pattern of activity, although the presentation of a carefully selected set of resources can be very helpful.

TABLE 6-5: Questions About Bulletin Boards and Usenet

Statements	*Agree strongly*	*Agree*	*No strong Opinion or Don't Know*	*Dis-agree*	*Dis-agree Strongly*	*Weighted Total*
	(1)	*(2)*	*(3)*	*(4)*	*(5)*	
Bulletin boards and Usenet newsgroups provide a good means for people to ask for help with problems.	11	31	15	5	2	2.31
Only the most extraverted students and staff post messages to bulletin Boards and newsgroups.	4	22	16	15	7	2.98
With a bulletin board everyone has a say, not just the most vocife-rous students.	9	31	15	8	1	2.39
I would like to take part in SLAPA class discussions on the SLAPA bulletin Board.	7	16	28	10	3	2.78

(Contd.)

Statements	*Agree strongly*	*Agree*	*No strong Opinion or Don't Know*	*Dis-agree*	*Dis-agree Strongly*	*Weighted Total*
	(1)	*(2)*	*(3)*	*(4)*	*(5)*	
It is good idea to post marks and other messages on the class bulletin board.	12	19	15	12	6	2.69
I find it difficult use a bulletin board.	4	10	17	16	15	3.45

Unfortunately, teachers must prepare the selection, which is probably presented as a set of links on a course-related page, and must spend considerable time and effort eliminating irrelevant and out-of-date items. A teacher approaching this task probably starts by using one of the major WWW search engines, but effective use of these is not simple, and no useful published guides help to use such services effectively.

TABLE 6-6: Questions About Internet Tools and Facilities

Statements	*Never*	*Rarely Tried It Once*	*Occasi-onally Less Than Once a Week*	*Frequently At Least Once a Week*	*Daily*	*Weighted Total*
	(1)	*(2)*	*(3)*	*(4)*	*(5)*	
I use elelctronic mail.	1	0	10	13	41	4.43
I use Telnet to login to remote computers.	7	5	15	17	21	3.62
I use FTP to transfer files to and from other computers.	11	6	20	16	10	3.13
I use anonymous FTP to obtain data and resources on Public archives.	20	10	16	11	6	2.57

Statements	*Never*	*Rarely Tried It Once*	*Occasionally Less Than Once a Week*	*Frequently At Least Once a Week*	*Daily*	*Weighted Total*
	(1)	*(2)*	*(3)*	*(4)*	*(5)*	
I use Archie to Locate resources on public archives.	33	15	7	5	3	1.89
I subscribe to one or more mailing list	30	12	10	3	8	2.16
I read one or more Usenet newsgroups.	18	12	19	5	12	2.71
I use Gopher to access remote resources.	31	16	9	4	3	1.92
I use WWW to access remote resources	3	4	12	24	17	3.80
I use WWW search engines to Locate remote resources.	6	4	14	20	20	3.69

The design of most search engines seems to owe little or nothing to library science and the skills acquired by librarians in organizing and cataloguing information. Unless students have plenty of time or have had considerable tutoring in using search engines effectively, they cannot be told to find out about something "on the Internet." Such an activity is likely to be frustrating and time wasting. Some search engines offer directories or hierarchies of directories; this approach is much closer to traditional classified library catalogues, but the selection of categories is sometimes rather arbitrary.

An institution of any reasonable size, it is probably helpful to identify an "expert" in the use of search engines. Such a person may well be a librarian or a person with training in librarianship. Alternatively, a teacher may choose to refer to an increasing number of Internet and WWW resource lists being prepared and published by educators. Even if these match the course structure and content, many doubts raised in the following paragraphs must apply to such lists.

Internet-based resources remain the property of their authors who can modify and remove them at any time, without previous notice. In marked contrast, library copies of resources remain in the library until removed by librarians. Once a resource has been transferred to a library, an author no longer has any control over it. There has been a little discussion about preparing a proper archive of the WWW, but as far as we know, there are no definite proposals.

There are also significant unresolved problems with intellectual property rights associated with material "published" on the WWW. The ease with which students can cut and paste material from their Web browsers into their own word processed assignments is also a cause for concern for teachers who may well inadvertently reward, as original, material that has been copied from an unfamiliar source. An important point for teachers to consider if they intend to require students to create Web pages as part of an assessment is the problem of plagiarism and the possibility of changes being made after handling dates. Once a Web page has been created, it is, in general, public and can be viewed and copied by anybody. Students who begin to work later than others can simply copy other people's already published results. We considered using special software to make automatic copies of pages for assessment purposes, but the software was not entirely successful. Another possibility would be to require students to submit the text of their pages via E-mail or on a floppy disk.

It is often difficult to judge the quality of a resource. With conventional published material, the reputation of the publisher and the mechanism of reviewing provide a reasonable guarantee of quality. There is no such mechanism on the WWW, and it is not always easy to tell whether a page is a result of peer group reviewed research or wild speculation perhaps supported by groups with extreme views.

There is an increasing tendency to use the WWW to publish material in a bewildering variety of formats, particularly under the banner of multimedia. This practice may be acceptable in a school or college context where it is possible to ensure that all machines are equipped with all the relevant viewers, but it can cause severe problems for home-based students who may not have the latest, fastest, most powerful machines.

The Way Forward — Interactive Use

Since the WWW was first created, it has had the ability to support interaction via hyperlinks. More recent versions have included the forms mechanism and the associated common gateway interface (CGI) mechanism that allows information gathered from remote browsers to be processed by local programs on the server computer, and thus provides a basis for client-server computing without the need to distribute special client programs. So-called sensitive maps provide another interactive mechanism. All these tools and methods seem to have been little used in education, possibly because of the significant computing skills needed.

The older and computationally simpler technique of multiple choice questions answered via selecting a hyperlink to one of several possible answers is also very rarely seen on the WWW. The problem here seems to be partly related to the difficulty of devising such tests, although some interesting automated approaches have been reported.

7

Products Successfully Promoted Via the Internet

The internet has the potential to reshape consumer buying patterns. Using a survey of 307 internet users, we explore four domains: consumer attitudes, internet experiences, demographics, and personality traits that may potentially influence consumers' online purchasing. Via a series of logistic regression analyses and a correspondence analysis, we identify some important influences. For instance, we find that those who have frequently requested product information and who are opinion leaders are relatively likely to engage in online purchasing. Managerial implications along with limitations of the study are provided.

"If I want to buy a pair of Nike sneakers, maybe I'll go to the Nike store, try them on and be in the environment. But I won't pay the premium Nike expects. I'll go home and order it online for a 50 percent discount.

The internet provides new ways for consumers to learn about and acquire products and services online. For instance, the internet provides consumers access to rich new information sources and thus helps them to make better-informed decisions. According to

Nielsen Media Research and Commerce Net (1999), worldwide internet users exceed 120 million. The value of electronic commerce transactions was approximately US $9 billion in 1997. In addition, Forrester Research expects that 60 million U.S. households will be online by 2003—an increase from 39 million in 1999-and that more internet users will access the web at higher speeds, enabling them to visit more information-oriented sites. Indeed, the internet is the driving force behind a transition from a static computer world to a space for human interactions.

To date, academic researchers have examined: online consumer behavior, internet advertising strategy, electronic marketing strategy, and the economics of the internet. There have been few studies that try to understand the types of purchases that consumers are willing to make on the internet and the factors related to such purchases. A major focus of this paper is to understand the internet as a communication medium and a platform for purchasing, and thus provide insight into developing advertising strategies and tactics.

In this study, our unit of analysis is the individual consumer. The dependent variable is whether or not that consumer has made purchases on the web (both in general and for nine specific product categories). The purpose of the present study is two-fold: (1) to identify factors that distinguish internet users who have made an internet purchase from those who have not, and (2) to identify the factors that distinguish internet users who have purchased specific products and services on the internet (e.g., books, computers, music, electronics). We explore four domains as possible determinants of internet purchases: attitudes (i.e., internet involvement, attitude toward internet advertisements), internet experiences (i.e., web use, product information requests), demographics (i.e., age, gender, education, household income), and personality variables (i.e., opinion leadership, risk awareness). These four domains are selected for study since they have proven to be important in explaining buyer behavior in conventional purchasing.

Our study is of interest to advertisers and their agencies for two reasons. First, some products may be more natural to promote on the internet than others. Second, knowing the profile of buyers in general, as well as buyers of particular products and services on the internet in particular, allows advertisers to effectively develop and target their advertising efforts. For example, purchasing computer products online is relatively risky because the cost of the product is relatively high, and there is no chance to try the product before buying. Therefore, consumers who purchase computer products online may be less risk-averse than those who do not. They may also tend to be opinion leaders, as much information is needed to make such a purchase. Here, we attempt to identify consumer factors that are associated with the likelihood of making purchases. In turn, these factors may be of use for creating segmentation and promotion strategies.

Conceptual Background

To marketers, the internet appears as a seemingly unlimited marketplace where billions of commercial messages travel along the huge commercial networks that make up only part of the internet. To consumers, the case for shopping on the internet is compelling. For instance, consumers can save time not only by shopping at a place where they have internet access but also by avoiding crowded shopping malls. In this section, we develop hypotheses relating explanatory domains (i.e., attitudes, internet experiences, demographics, and personality traits) to the likelihood of making purchases on the web. Although these hypotheses address general online purchasing, we will subsequently explore them in specific product and service contexts, as well as in general.

Attitudes

We explore how web purchasing is related to consumers attitude toward internet advertising in general and degree of general involvement with the internet. Marketers have started considering the internet as an important medium for their promotional activities. According to Forrester Research, online advertising expenditure reached $5.4 billion in 2000 from $2.8 billion in 1999. Further, spending on this medium is projected to be $22 billion by 2004, a little over 8 percent of total U.S. advertising spending. Although the average click-through rate hovers at about 0.5 percent to 2 percent, banner advertising has been the most dominant advertising technique online. As consumers are exposed to internet advertisements, they develop an "attitude" toward the internet as an advertising medium. The more that a consumer accepts the internet as a legitimate medium for commercial communication, the more likely that consumer is to purchase goods and services over the internet.

Consumer involvement has been defined in many different ways and can be operationalized as a perceptual or attitudinal factor. We are interested in consumers' degree of involvement with the internet (as a communication medium) and anticipate that internet-involved consumers will be more likely to purchase than those with low-involvement levels. Thus our first research hypothesis is:

> H1: *Positive attitudes (i.e., internet involvement and attitudes toward internet advertising) will increase the likelihood that a consumer will make an online purchase.*

Internet Experiences

In contrast to traditional shopping activities, consumers need to acquire some basic internet-related skills (e.g., ability to use browsers, email) to shop online. Thus, the lack of internet skills may be a barrier for some consumers who desire to shop online. For example, according to Matrix Information and Directory Services (American Demographics, 1997), almost 28 million Americans can use the internet for email, but fewer than half of those can access interactive services on the World Wide Web. Consumers must become accustomed to the procedures for ordering online. They will also feel comfortable knowing that they can negotiate the procedures for post-purchase services.

As consumers surf the internet and request product information, for instance, they are likely to receive commercial solicitations and promotions. According to the Pew Research Center, 46 percent of internet users use email every day, and 36 percent of email users receive unwanted messages, 72 percent of which are sales solicitations. Just as in the traditional business world, increased exposure to the internet and online marketing efforts (e.g., commercial websites) increases consumers' likelihood of online purchases. Based on the above discussion, we propose the following research hypothesis:

H2: *Internet experiences (i.e., internet use, product information requests) are positively related to the likelihood that a consumer will make an online purchase.*

In one part of this hypothesis, we are stating that internet experiences lead to acquired skills. As a consumer gains experience in a related activity (e.g., ability to understand security issues in online purchases), then this experience increases the likelihood of an online purchase. In the other part, we are stating that product information requests lead to solicitation which, in turn, leads to buying.

Demographics

Advertisers view demographic variables as viable segmenting tools, and they see demographics as providing useful explanations of buyer behavior. Internet users tend to be young, male, well educated, and tend to have above-average income. However, Donthu and Garcia report that internet shoppers are older and have higher income than traditional retail consumers. That is, low income may serve as a barrier that restricts the ability of young consumers to make purchases online. Based on this preliminary profile of internet users, we propose that household income, age, gender, and education status will have an effect on the likelihood of internet purchasing.

H3: *Demographic variables (i.e., age, gender, household income, education status) will be related to online purchasing.*

Personality Variables

Personality variables explain a modest amount of variance in consumers' purchases outside of cyberspace. We expect two variables to play an important role in the virtual world: opinion leadership and risk aversion. Social factors are important to consider when trying to understand internet purchasing. Consumers are likely to use interpersonal sources for purchasing in a retail environment. The extant studies suggest that a considerable percentage of consumers are likely to seek information and advice from "market mavens," among other influences for buying products and services. Interpersonal sources may be more important than marketing-controlled sources. Such reliance on interpersonal sources has the potential to be even more important in electronic buying environments, since, as discussed earlier, electronic purchasing requires sophisticated, knowledge-based skills (e.g., how to search, where to buy) than does traditional shopping.

The concept of risk is important for understanding how internet consumers make choices. Individuals face risk when a decision, action, or behavior can lead to different possible outcomes. An important aspect of online risk is uncertainty or ambiguity. Shopping environments on the internet may be uncertain for the majority of online shoppers, especially if they are novices. For instance, a major drawback of electronic business is the inability of the buyer to physically inspect a product before buying. Consumers can try on clothes in a store before they make a final decision. However, this is not the case on the internet. They have to assume more risk when purchasing products on the internet as opposed to buying in the mall, Further, uncertainty may become higher when products and services are highly involving (e.g., jewelry, computer, education). We expect that risk takers are more likely to engage in online purchasing than their counterparts. Based on our literature review, we propose the following hypothesis incorporating our two personality variables:

> **H4:** *Personality variables (i.e., product opinion leadership, risk taking propensities) will be positively related to online purchasing.*

Method Sample

In order to investigate our research hypotheses, a web-based chatting server was chosen to obtain a sample of internet users. Respondents were contacted using email and were invited to participate in an online survey. Access to the survey website was included in the email correspondence. Email invitations to participate in the survey were sent every three hours to all those using the chatting server at that time. As an incentive to participate in the survey, email recipients were told that they would be entered in a drawing for four prizes (i.e., four video phones enabling visual chatting), valued at approximately $100 each upon completion of the survey. This procedure was repeated every day for two weeks, generating 307 usable responses for the study.

Measures

Internet purchasing. Respondents were first asked whether they have bought products and/or services on the internet. The 142 respondents (46.3 percent) who had made a purchase online were also questioned specifically regarding whether they had purchased: (a) books, information, or magazines; (b) communications services (e.g., internet phone services); (c) computer-related products and services; (d) education; (e) electronics; (f) entertainment; (g) internet-related products and services; (h) music and videos; and (i) travel and vacations (e.g., airplane tickets). As presented in Table 1, computer-related products and services (31.6 percent, n = 97) and books, information, and magazines (26.7 percent, n = 82) were identified as the most frequently purchased products, whereas electronics and entertainment were least frequently purchased online (12.1 percent, n = 37 for both categories).

These nine product categories were selected for a variety of reasons. First, both products and services are represented. Second, all nine categories are regularly offered for sale online. Finally there is considerable variability in the frequency of online purchasing in these categories. Attitudes. In order to explore consumer attitudes, two constructs are operationalized: attitude toward internet advertising and consumer involvement with the internet. A general advertising attitude scale was used to evaluate consumers' attitudes toward internet advertisements. Subjects were asked to rate nine items, using a 7-point semantic differential scale (e.g., untrustworthy/trustworthy, not credible/credible) in the context of the following question: "What is your general attitude toward internet advertising (e.g., banner advertising) compared to traditional advertising (e.g., TV and radio advertising, magazine, and newspaper advertising)?" All nine items were summed to calculate an aggregate measure. Higher scores reflect a more favorable attitude toward internet advertising.

A number of scales to measure involvement have been designed and used in marketing literature. However, most of the extant scales measure "object (i.e., product)" involvement. Here, we define internet involvement as a person's consistent "interest" in the internet. Thus, our operationalization of involvement is quite different from an object-based involvement, in that object-oriented involvement typically requires inherent needs and values of an object. Two questions were devised to measure consumer involvement with the internet: (1) "How interested are you in the subject of the internet?" and (2) "How frequently do you find yourself thinking about the internet?" Each question used a 7-point scale and two bipolar adjectives (not at all interested/very interested and never/very often, respectively). Reliability of the scale was examined by calculating the correlation between the two items ($r = .35$ $p < .05$). These two ratings were summed to produce a single score. Higher scores on the scale represent higher involvement with the internet.

Internet experiences. We explored two behavioral or experiential components: internet use and product information requests. First, consumers' internet usage was measured using two questions: "Approximately how long do you use the internet on a typical day?" and "Approximately how long did you use the internet yesterday?" The majority of the respondents (60.3 percent, $n = 186$) use the internet between one and five hours per day. Correlation between the two items is high and significant (r .81, $p < .05$). These two items were summed to produce a single measure.

Respondents were asked two questions about product-information-seeking behavior: "Approximately how often have you requested information about products from companies in your country via the internet?" and "Approximately how often have you requested information about products from companies in a foreign country via the internet?" As anticipated, these two items showed a significant positive correlation ($r = .48$, $p < .05$) and were added to produce a single measure. Also, 61.3 percent of respondents ($n = 185$) requested product information from firms in their countries more than one time, whereas 46.3 percent (n 139) did so more than once from companies in foreign countries.

Demographics

Four demographic variables (i.e., age, gender, household income, and education) were included in the survey. The majority of respondents were between 16 and 40 years old (79.8 percent), are male (70 percent), and reported having at least a college education (82 percent). Over half (52 percent) were employed full time. The results agree with previous research findings that many internet users are highly educated.

It is well known that respondents are likely to overestimate their absolute income. Thus, we asked two income questions using a comparative 11-point scale: "What is your household income per month compared to your country's average household income?" anchored by lowest/highest.

Personality variables. Two personality traits were measured as possible in online purchasing: (1) risk-taking propensity and (2) opinion leadership. In both cases, a sum of individual scale rating was used to calculate a single measure.

Zuckerman's Sensation Seeking scale was used to assess consumers' risk-taking tendencies. Thirteen items were randomly chosen from the original scale for ease of implementation. The scale employs a 7-point Likert-type scale anchored by strongly disagree/ strongly agree. An acceptable reliability estimate was obtained (Cronbach's alpha = .89). Higher scores on the scale represent higher levels of risk-taking tendency.

In order to measure consumers' opinion leadership in the marketplace, five items from Feick and Price's (1987) Market Maven Scale were employed. The scale measures not only opinion leaders' general influence on knowledge and expertise but also consumers' expertise in the marketplace. This 7-point Likert-type scale is anchored by strongly disagree/strongly agree. High reliability was achieved (alpha = .90). Higher scores represent higher tendencies to diffuse knowledge about the marketplace.

Analysis and Results

In order to explore the hypotheses, a series of logistic regression analyses were conducted. Internet purchasing results (i.e., Yes or No) were used as dichotomous dependent variables, and ten variables from the four domains (i.e., attitude, internet experience, demographics, and personality) were the candidate independent variables. First, the effects of the four factors on general internet purchasing were examined, and then the nine individual product categories were studied analogously.

In order to evaluate the models, traditional likelihood ratio tests of significance, concordant and discordant rates, and variable odds ratios are used. The study focuses on the significance of the four domains, and then the individual variables that comprise these domains, not on developing predictive models. For each domain, we first conduct multiple logistic regression analysis to determine whether the domain influences online purchasing. If the result is not significant, then the domain does not appear to be related to online buying. If the result is statistically significant, then the domain is related to online buying. Further, individual logistic regressions are applied to those domain variables that are not significant in the model. This mitigates the possible problem of multicollinearity, whereby influential variables are considered unimportant because their coefficients are insignificant in the multiple regression model.

In addition, having identified possible variables that are important in explaining online purchases, a perceptual map for the nine product categories is developed using multiple correspondence analysis. This analysis is particularly interesting to advertising practitioners since mapping consumers' internet purchasing behaviors can provide some insights for their online advertising strategies and implementations.

Attitude (H1)

The aggregate model is statistically significant for overall internet purchasing. However, Hi is supported only for the internet involvement variable. The concordant rate is 59.8 percent. In other words, for about 60 percent of all the possible pairs of actual buyers and non-buyers, the calculated (by the model) probability of being a buyer is higher for the actual buyer than non-buyer. The model is also significant for seven of the nine product and service categories investigated. The aggregate model is not significant in the case of entertainment and music.

Internet involvement seems to have a large impact on web purchasing. Overall internet buying is positively affected by consumers' involvement with the internet. The odds for purchasing in general (overall) increase by a factor of 1.18 for one unit increase of consumers internet involvement in the measurement scale. Except for the entertainment and music categories, internet involvement is found to have significantly positive effects on internet buying.

Although consumers' attitudes toward online advertisements do not play a significant role in the aggregate model, the results suggest that attitude toward internet advertising has a positive effect on purchasing books, computers, education, electronic goods, internet-related products and services, and travel.

Internet Experience (H2)

The aggregate model is again statistically significant for general online purchasing as well as all nine purchase categories in the internet experience domain. "Product information requests" was statistically significant for the overall purchasing model as well as for all nine individual categories. In particular, there is a 35.5 percent increase in the odds ratio for purchasing computer-related products for a one unit increase of the seeking-product-information measure.

Although "internet use" was not statistically significant in the overall model, this variable was significant in seven of the nine categories. It is interesting to note that consumers' use of the internet is highly related to purchasing internet related products and services. In summary, H2 is fully supported for product-information requests over the web and partially supported for internet use.

Demographics (H3)

The demographic domain provides a significant model for overall purchasing, and purchasing in all but the entertainment and music categories. Gender and income are the primary influential demographic factors, and h3 is generally supported for these two factors. When gender is significant, men are more likely to purchase online than women. In particular, the odds for overall purchase online are 2.4 times higher for males than for females. The impact of gender is seen in all of the nine product categories except entertainment and music, but even in these two categories, the non significant coefficient is positive.

Household income is also found to be a significant positive determinant of internet purchasing overall and in eight of the nine (music excluded) categories. A one-unit increase of the household income measure results in at least a 17 percent increase in the odds for internet purchasing in all product categories except for music.

It is interesting to note that age and education are found to be weak influencers. For instance, higher educational status leads to higher web purchasing in only communications and travel. Only purchasing computer equipment online is positively related with age. However, this relationship is weak since a one-unit increase of age (5 years) creates only a 12.7 percent increase in the odds for online computer purchasing.

Personality (H4)

The personality domain provides a significant model for overall purchasing, and for purchasing in seven of the nine categories (communications and music excluded). Of the personality variables, opinion leadership is the most important variable in explaining consumers' web purchasing. The results suggest that overall internet purchasing is enhanced by a high score for opinion leadership, and the same can be said for two-thirds of the specific categories. A one-unit increase of opinion leadership leads to a 7.8 percent increase in the odds for overall web purchasing. This impact is consistent through the individual product categories except for communications, entertainment, and music.

We find that consumers' risk-taking tendencies are positively related to overall online purchasing, although the impact is weak (odds ratio of 1.016 or 1.6 percent slope). Also, online purchasing of education and entertainment products are positively influenced by consumers' risk–taking propensities. Thus, H4 is generally supported in the case of opinion leadership.

Dimensional Characteristics of Nine Categories

Whether or not respondents have purchased online in the nine products and service categories provides the basis for the map. The map appears to portray two dimensions—"the degree of information required to purchase" and "popularity of purchasing on the internet." Books and computer-related products are positioned in the high information and high popularity zone. Music and electronics appear to anchor the popularity dimension.

Entertainment products are perceived as relatively low information and low popularity. Following is a discussion of the notion of such a segmentation of internet products and services in detail.

Discussion

Using an internet-user sample of 307, we evaluated four possible domains (i.e., consumer attitudes, internet experiences, demographics, and personality traits) that may influence consumers' web purchasing. From a series of logistic regression analyses and a multiple correspondence analysis, we find some evidence that our four groups of variables influence patterns of internet purchases.

Factors Influencing Web Purchasing

High involvement is related to the overall internet purchase and to most of the individual products and services, except for entertainment and music. However, attitude toward online advertisements is not related to overall internet purchasing and is a weaker variable in explaining consumers' web purchasing in specific categories than internet involvement. One reason for this may be the fact that attitudes toward internet advertising in general were measured.

Nonetheless, these findings provide interesting facts to advertising practitioners. Although there has been an endless debate about whether advertising ultimately creates sales or just functions to increase top-of-mind awareness, the research outcomes suggest that web purchasing may not be considerably enhanced by consumers' mere exposure to internet advertisements which, in turn, may generate certain positive attitudes to web advertising. Rather, online consumers' buying behavior may be rooted in their self-generated interests with the subjects of the web before they surf the online marketplace. Thus, commercials about products and services using traditional mass media (e.g., TV) may be helpful to trigger online consumers who have consistent interests with the internet to purchase these products and services online.

As far as consumers' web experience is concerned, consumers who frequently access the internet engage in online purchasing more often for books, computer products, education, electronic goods, entertainment, internet-related products, and travel than consumers who access the internet less frequently. Our results also suggest that consumers' online experiences in product-related issues largely affect product purchasing incidence. In other words, we find that consumers who frequently seek product information online are more likely to engage in web purchasing. This trend is confirmed through overall purchase and all nine individual product categories. This is important to note for marketing practitioners. Unlike traditional media (e.g., television, radio), the internet allows consumers to select and choose what they want exposure to. Thus, "pull" strategies (e.g., prepared rich information about products and services on the web) may be more effective on the internet than "push" efforts (e.g., consumer promotion s) since web consumers voluntarily tend to explore a specific site. To advertisers, a rational (contextual) appeal in their advertisements may be more powerful on the internet than an emotional appeal to fulfill consumers' need for cognition.

Unlike previous findings, we find that age does not play an important role in web purchasing, except in the case of computer products. Regarding gender differences in web purchasing, men are more likely than women to be online buyers. As anticipated, higher household income creates more frequent internet buying in most product categories. Education is not a particularly good predictor in many categories, as well as overall. One reason for age and education not being good predictors may be that, with more and more people "surfing" the internet, the internet may have shifted from the stage of early adoption (i.e., a new medium) to the stage of growth (i.e., near mass medium).

Our results suggest that opinion leadership is the most important variable among other personality components. That is, those who have high opinion leadership are more likely to purchase diverse products and services online than their counterparts. The positive relationship between opinion leadership and internet purchasing is natural. Innovative trendsetters are, by definition, the early adopters of new technology and there is a likely correlation between trend-setting and opinion leadership.

Also, web purchasing to varying degrees is more risky than purchasing in traditional retail environments (e.g., no instant trials, security of transactions). Hence, risk-takers should be more likely to purchase online than the counterpart consumers. Our results indicate that risk taking tendency is positively linked to overall web purchasing and purchasing in several individual product categories (i.e., education, entertainment).

Segmentation of Web Purchasing

Having identified some possible variables that influence consumers' web purchasing, it is beneficial for advertisers to know how online purchasing can be segmented based on consumers' buying patterns in the nine product and service categories. Consequently, the research findings provide insights for advertisers and advertising agency practitioners in terms of a segmentation strategy of web products and services. We identify and label two main segmenting dimensions: (1) depth of information needed (low versus high) and (2) popularity of online purchasing of products and services (low versus high). These two dimensions produce four segments (quadrants such as Q1, Q2, Q3, and Q4) based on the poles of each dimension. However, caution must be exercised in interpreting the degree of information-needed axes. For instance, products and services (i.e., music and entertainment in the study) on the low end of the spectrum are not necessarily purchased without careful thought and deliberation.

Music products are among the most popular types of products for purchasing online and score on low information required (Q1). This is interesting to advertisers. In the 1980s, music manufacturers enhanced exposure to the product through radio and then sold it through retailers like Tower Records and Warehouse. However, over the past few years, new internet music startups like CD Now, N2K, MP3.com, and Liquid Audio have revolutionized the way the industry and consumers transact. Without going to retail shops (e.g., Circuit City), buyers can now sample music on the internet. Via numerous product trials and free information for the product on the web that are not typically available offline, customers may already have enough knowledge before they make a decision to purchase the product. This product category may be in a cash-cow stage with the advent of the internet. We believe that frequent advertising campaigns focusing on consumer promotions (e.g., free product trials) are essential for music products on the web.

Interestingly, entertainment products and services are positioned in the fourth quadrant (Q4). This online purchasing category is categorized as low information needed and low degree of popularity in consumers' minds. Thus, advertisers may want to focus mainly on triggering consumers' buying motivations in their advertising campaign since sales of the product (or service) category may be enhanced by buyers' short-term curiosities (e.g., purchasing and participating in online gaming and gambling). For instance, an increasing number of gaming sites use their internet advertisements with a motivation-driven advertising campaign (e.g., free online game services for basic service lines, one-month free membership).

Books and computers are positioned in a high-information required and a popular segment (Q2). Therefore, advertising practitioners may want to use internet and offline print media rather than TV or radio to provide information and stimulate interest. In particular, regarding computer products, running advertisements in specialized magazines (e.g., PC Magazine) might be much more effective. Detailed information on banner advertisements can help increase sales of these categories. However, general print media (e.g., newspapers and magazines such as Business Week) also help to increase buyers' perception of computer purchases online since the media has been traditionally considered to be effective medium for high-involvement consumers. Also, the use of offline communication may be helpful. For instance, Gateway (www.gateway.com), one of the biggest online computer firms, has recently introduced an offline shop to provide more information so that consumers can try their products and services before they order on line. As has been known from previous findings, books are perceived as a popular and high-information-required product category. We believe that such a product category thrives on the integration of online (e.g., for information) and offline (e.g., for keeping popularity) advertising campaigns. The integrated campaign works to build both brand image and sales over the long term.

Finally, education, travel, internet, communication, and electronic products and services are high information-needed and low popularity categories (Q3). They also score low in purchasing on the web. Web consumers may try to seek relatively high information to purchase in these categories. Thus, some aided consumer communications on the web (e.g., an extensive illustration of products and services on purchasing sites along with prior banner advertisements) are necessary. Also, installation of chatting services for the purpose of customer service may help consumers who need more information because managers can interactively provide customized information as needed.

Limitations and Conclusion

Limitations in interpreting the outcomes of the present study should be noted. The sample used in the study was selected from web chatters. Hence, respondents may already possess more technical skills for using the internet than general internet users. They may also have more experience with internet activities than general internet users. However, skewing the sample to internet "savvy" consumers likely only inflates the purchasing percentages. It is highly unlikely that the results and patterns observed are distorted. Further, the sample represents the universe that is gradually evolving.

Now, more than 44.4 percent of U.S. households can surf the web. The internet provides opportunities for borderless marketing and facilitates economic transactions. Thus, future research may want to look at the transnational effects of the internet on global marketing. For instance, what are the particular products and services that are successfully sold on the web around the world? More interestingly, what are the differences between business transactions on a domestic website and a foreign internet site, both from marketers' and consumers' perspectives? Consumer ethnocentrism may be one possible factor to consider when investigating the global impact of the web. For instance, global marketers may have to adopt heterogeneous strategies to be successful on the internet. Although consumers' chatting behavior was not the focus in web purchasing in the present study, many firms have started adopting chatting functions on their sites and future studies should investigate the impact of these service s. For example, installation of chatting on the web is believed to increase online transactions.

Logistic Regression Analysis for Attitude Domain (H1)

InDependent\Dependent (a) (142/48.3%) (b) (82/26.7%)

Aggregate Model

Internet Involvement .189 * .236 *
(1.177) (c) (1.225)
Attitude toward Internet .041 .170 *
Ads (1.007) (1.030)

Model Fit

Likelihood Ratio ([chi square]) 10.012 (2) * 19.184 (2) *
Concordant 59.8 65.1
Discordant 39.3 34.1
Testing Insignificant
Variables
Internet Involvement

Attitude toward Internet .098
Ads (1.017)
Summary (d)
Internet Involvement * *
Attitude toward
Internet Ads * *
Communications Computer
Independent\Dependant (40/13.0%) (97/31.6%)

Aggregate Model

Internet Involvement .225 * .238 *
(1.214) (1.228)
Attitude toward Internet -.056 .098
Ads (.990) (1.017)

Model Fit

Likelihood Ratio ([chi square]) 4.616 (2) * 15.654 (2) *
Concordant 59.0 63.0
Discordant 39.6 36.0
Testing Insignificant

Variables
Internet Involvement

Attitude toward Internet .007 .170 *
Ads (1.001) (1.030)
Summary (d)
Internet Involvement * *
Attitude toward
Internet Ads *
Education Electronic Entertainment
Independent\Dependant (45/14.7%) (39/12.7%) (37/12.1%)

Aggregate Model

Internet Involvement .184 * .154 .111
(1.172) (1.142) (1.101)
Attitude toward Internet .109 .139 .028
Ads (1.019) (1.025) (1.005)

Model Fit

Likelihood Ratio ([chi square]) 6.758 (2) * 6.007 (2) * 1.523 (2)
Concordant 60.0 60.9 54.3
Discordant 38.8 37.4 42.6
Testing Insignificant
Variables
Internet Involvement .203 *
(1.191)

Attitude toward Internet .168 * .191 *
Ads (1.030) (1.034)
Summary (d)
Internet Involvement * *
Attitude toward
Internet Ads * *
Internet Music Travel
Independent\Dependant (37/12.1%) (62/20.2%) (46/15.0%)

Aggregate Model

Internet Involvement .193 * -.116 .192 *
(1.181) (.905) (1.180)

Attitude toward Internet .157 * .094 .117
Ads (1.028) (1.017) (1.021)

Model Fit

7.645 (2) *
Likelihood Ratio ([chi square]) 9.232 (2) * 2.454 (2)
Concordant 63.7 54.2 61.8
Discordant 34.5 44.0 36.9
Testing Insignificant
Variables
Internet Involvement

Attitude toward Internet .180 *
Ads – – (1.032)
Summary (d)
Internet Involvement * *
Attitude toward
Internet Ads * *

(a) Parameter estimates are standardized
(b) The number of online buyers in each category and the corresponding percentage of the base of n = 307.
(c) Odds ratio for event
(d) Summary findings incorporate results from both the aggregate model and individual models testing insignificant variables.

* Significant at $p < .05$ (one-tailed tests were performed for regression coefficients since our hypothesis

Logistic Regression Analysis for Experience Domain (H2)

Overall Books
Independent\Dependent (a)(142/46.3%) (b) (82/26.7%)

Aggregate Model

Internet Use .041 .130 *
(1.023) (c) (1.075)

Product Information .424 * .356 *
(1.267) (1.220)

Model Fit

Likelihood Ratio ([chi square]) 35.861 (2) * 29.274 (2) *
Concordant 70.2 69.3
Discordant 28.5 29.6
Testing Insignificant
Variables
.061

Internet Use (1.034)
Product Information
Summary (d)
Internet Use *
Product Information * *
Communications Computer
Independent\Dependent (40/13.0%) (97/31.6%)

Aggregate Model
Internet Use .107 .288 *
(1.061) (1.174)
Product Information .349 * .545 *
(1.215) (1.355)

Model Fit

Likelihood Ratio ([chi square]) 17.012 (2) * 70.729 (2) *
Concordant 69.4 78.1
Discordant 29.3 21.1
Testing Insignificant
Variables
.137

Internet Use — (1.080)
Product Information
Summary (d)
Internet Use *
Product Information * *
Education Electronic

Independent\Dependent (45/14.7%) (39/12.7%)

Aggregate Model

Internet Use .207 * .218 *
(1.122) (1.130)
Product Information .259 * .434 *
(1.210) (1.274)

Model Fit

Likelihood Ratio ([chi square]) 21.506 (2) * 28.101 (2) *
Concordant 70.8 73.6
Discordant 27.7 24.1
Testing Insignificant
Variables

Internet Use — —
Product Information — —
Summary (d)
Internet Use * *
Product Information * *
Entertainment Internet
Independent\Dependent (37/12.1%) (37/12.1%)

Aggregate Model

Internet Use .200 * .327 *
(1.118) (1.200)
Product Information .285 * .341 *
(1.172) (1.210)

Model Fit

Likelihood Ratio ([chi square]) 13.953 (2) * 26.070 (2) *
Concordant 68.5 72.5
Discordant 30.0 25.8
Testing Insignificant
Variables

Internet Use
Product Information

Summary (d)
Internet Use * *
Product Information * *
Music Travel
Independent\Dependent (62/20.2%) (46/15.0%)

Aggregate Model

Internet Use .111 .216 *
(1.064) (1.128)
Product Information .235 * .398 *
(1.140) (1.249)

Model Fit

Likelihood Ratio ([chi square]) 11.931 (2) * 27.780 (2) *
Concordant 63.9 72.4
Discordant 34.2 26.1
Testing Insignificant
Variables
.130

Internet Use
(1.075)
Product Infc⁻mation
Summary (d)
Internet Use *
Product Information * *

(a) Parameter estimates are standardized.

(b) The number of online buyers in each category and the corresponding percentage of tile base of n = 307.

(c) Odds ratio for event

(d) Summary findings incorporate results from both the aggregate model and individual models testing insignificant variables.

* Significant at $p < .05$ (one-tailed tests were performed for regression coefficients since our hypotheses suggest a positive (or negative) coefficient).

Logistic Regression Analysis for Demographic Domain (H3)

Independent\ Overall Books
Dependent (a) (142/46.3%) (b) (82/26.7%)

Aggregate Model

Age -.089 .007
(0.930) (c) (1.006)

Gender .222 * .205 *
(2.394) (2.241)

Household Income .191 * .282 *
(1.188) (1.289)

Education -.007 .127
(0.990) (1.190)

Model Fit

Likelihood Ratio ([chi square]) 21.333 (4) * 22.944 (4) *
Concordant 64.2 66.0
Discordant 35.0 33.1

Testing Insignificant
Variables
Age -.015 .072
(.988) (1.060)

Gender — —

Household Income — —

Education .027 .027
(1.037) (1.037)
Summary (d)
Age
Gender * *
Household Income * *
Education

Independent\ Communications Computer
Dependent (40/13.0%) (97/31.6%)

Aggregate Model

Age .065 .079
(1.054) (1.068)

Gender .152 .339 *
(1.819) (3.806)

Household Income .201 * .176 *
(1.199) (1.172)

Education .150 .062
(1.227) (1:089)

Model Fit

Likelihood Ratio ([chi square]) 11.520 (4) * 32.747 (4) *
Concordant 66.3 69.0
Discordant 32.6 30.3
Testing Insignificant
Variables
Age .111 .148 *
(1.094) (1.127)

Gender .205 * —
(2.240)

Household Income — —
Education .186 * .099
(1.289) (1.145)
Summary (d)
Age *
Gender * *
Household Income * *
Education *
Independent\ Education Electronic Dependent (45/14.7%)
(39/12.7%)

Aggregate Model

Age -.001 .023
(0.999) (1.019)

Gender .162 .348 *
(1.896) (3.942)

Household Income .248 * .133
(1.251) (1.127)

Education .030 .007
(1.042) (1.009)

Model Fit

Likelihood Ratio ([chi square]) 11.325 (4) * 12.044 (4) *
Concordant 63.3 65.2
Discordant 34.8 33.5
Testing Insignificant
Variables
Age .058 .085
(1.048) (1.072)

Gender .203 * –
(2.221)

Household Income – .180 *
(1.176)

Education .069 .042
(1.098) (1.059)
Summary (d)
Age
Gender **
Household Income **
Education
Independent\ Entertainment Internet
Dependent (37/12.1%) (37/12.1%)

Aggregate Model

Age -.139 .012
(0.893) (1.010)

Gender .177 .276 *
(2.010) (2.971)

Household Income .208 * .326 *
(1.207) (1.341)

Education -.101 -.124
(0.871) (0.844)

Model Fit

Likelihood Ratio ([chi square]) 9.012 (4) 12.205 (4) *
Concordant 64.0 64.8
Discordant 34.9 34.0
Testing Insignificant
Variables
Age — .068
(1.057)

Gender — —

Household Income — —

Education — -.112
(.859)

Summary (d)
Age
Gender *

Household Income * *
Education
Independent\ Music Travel
Dependent (62/20.2%) (46/15.0%)

Aggregate Model

Age -.087 .072
(.932) (1.060)

Gender .063 .204 *
(1.283) (2.233)

Household Income .123 .191 *
(1.117) (1.188)

Education 037 .163
(1.052) (1.250)

Model Fit

Likelihood Ratio ([chi square]) 4.061 (4) 15.151 (4) *
Concordant 56.3 66.5
Discordant 42.1 32.2
Testing Insignificant
Variables
Age – .122
(1.104)

Gender – –

Household Income – –

Education – .199 *
(1.313)

Summary (d)
Age
Gender *
Household Income *
Education *

(a) Parameter estimates are standardized.

(b) The number of online buyers in each category and the corresponding percentage of the base of n = 307.]

(c) Odds ratio for event

(d) Summary findings incorporate results from both the aggregate model and individual models testing insignificant variables.

* Significant at $p < .05$ (one-tailed tests were performed for regression coefficients since our hypotheses suggest a positive (or negative) coefficient).

Logistic Regression Analysis for Personality Domain (H4)

Independent\ Overall Books

Dependent (a) (142/46.3%) (b) (82/26.7%)

Aggregate Model

Opinion Leadership .322 * .381 *
(1.078) (c) (1.093)

Risk-Taking .071 -.010
(1.008) (0.999)

Model Fit

Likelihood Ratio ([chi square]) 26.482 (2) * 26.871 (2) *
Concordant 66.2 67.9
Discordant 33.4 31.5
Testing Insignificant
Variables

Opinion Leadership — —
Risk-Taking .148 * .079
(1.016) (1.009)

Summary (d)
Opinion Leadership * *
Risk-Taking *

Independent\ Communications Computer
Dependent (40/13.0%) (97/31.6%)

Aggregate Model

Opinion Leadership .132 .466 *
(1.031) (1.115)

Risk-Taking -.056 -.025
(0.994) (0.997)

Model Fit
Likelihood Ratio ([chi square]) 1.923 (2) 38.612 (2) *
Concordant 56.2 70.9
Discordant 41.9 28.8
Testing Insignificant
Variables

Opinion Leadership
Risk-Taking — .081
(1.009)

Summary (d)
Opinion Leadership *
Risk-Taking
Independent\ Education Electronic
Dependent (45/14.7%) (39/12.7%)

Aggregate Model

Opinion Leadership .360 * .529 *
(1.087) (1.131)

Risk-Taking .104 .001
(1.011) (1.000)

Model Fit

Likelihood Ratio ([chi square]) 17.333 (2) * 25.512 (2) *
Concordant 68.3 71.7
Discordant 31.0 25.3

Testing Insignificant
Variables

Opinion Leadership — —
Risk-Taking .184 * .111
(1.020) (1.012)

Summary (d)
Opinion Leadership * *
Risk-Taking *

Independent\ Entertainment Internet
Dependent (37/12.1%) (37/12.1%)

Aggregate Model

Opinion Leadership .067 .247 *
(1.016) (1.059)

Risk-Taking .265 * .021
(1.030) (1.002)

Model Fit

Likelihood Ratio ([chi square]) 7.873 (2) * 7.290 (2) *
Concordant 63.5 61.6
Discordant 35.6 37.6
Testing Insignificant
Variables

Opinion Leadership .131 –
(1.031)
Risk-Taking – .081
(1.009)

Summary (d)
Opinion Leadership *
Risk-Taking *

Independent\ Music Travel
Dependent (62/20.2%) (46/15.0%)

Aggregate Model

Opinion Leadership .101 .458 *
(1.024) (1.113)

Risk-Taking .074 .004
(1.008) (1.000)

Model Fit

Likelihood Ratio ([chi square]) 3.053 (2) 22.901 (2) *
Concordant 55.8 70.1
Discordant 42.8 27.5
Testing Insignificant
Variables

Opinion Leadership – –

Risk-Taking – .103
(1.011)

Summary (d)
Opinion Leadership *
Risk-Taking

(a) Parameter estimates are standardized.
(b) The number of online buyers in each category and the corresponding percentage of the base of n = 307.
(c) Odds ratio for event
(d) Summary findings incorporate results from both the aggregate model
and individual models testing insignificant variables.

* Significant at $p < .05$ (one-tailed tests were performed for regression coefficients since our hypotheses suggest a positive (or negative) coefficient).

8

ADVERTISING ON THE INTERNET

Definition of Advertising

Paid, nonpersonal communication through various media by business firms, nonprofit organizations, and individuals who are in some way identified in the advertising message and who hope to inform or persuade members of a particular audience.

In the past five years, we have seen the Internet increase 25-fold. According to January 1998 estimates, the commercial domain is the largest domain on the Internet with 28% of all Internet hosts. Moreover, the commercial domain is by far the largest and fastest growing on the World Wide Web with an estimated 63% of all sites on the Web. It appears that businesses are increasingly taking part in the new marketing forum available in cyberspace. Yet, many companies are growing disillusioned with the commercial possibilities of online advertising, and some have suggested that the Internet is better suited for interpersonal communication and personal sites rather than commercial sites. Executives are questioning whether the potential of the Internet is real or just hype, and some companies are considering decreasing or removing their investment in online advertising. Questions remain, however, whether these online businesses are currently taking advantage of the Internet's capabilities and hence its potential benefits. Moreover, are these businesses integrating their online marketing strategy effectively with other traditional advertising media? Or, are their online advertising strategies actually precluding them from attaining the potential benefits of online advertising? Our research attempts to address these questions.

Potential Benefits of Advertising Online

For businesses, advertising on the Internet offers potential benefits that are not available through traditional advertising media. This new medium has caught the attention of advertising and marketing experts in several fields, and a range of research has just begun to highlight the differences between online and traditional advertising.

Information Richness. The broadcast nature of television, radio, billboard, and print constrain a traditional advertisement to one short, memorable message. With the Internet, the advertising message is no longer so constrained. The Internet allows for communicating to consumers substantially more content-rich product information.

Ease of Updating. Maintaining an online ad is less costly than maintaining traditional ads and lacks the delays of other media. Furthermore, online information can be quickly and easily changed and updated.

Brand Information. Whereas certain brand-relevant information is often considered too frivolous, given the space limitations of a traditional ad, the online ad can contain more brand-relevant information important for building brand image. For instance, the site can contain trivia about the company, provide detailed information about the organizations it sponsors, and link to interesting image-related sites.

Data Collection. In exchange for this information and/or other product incentives, the company can easily and inexpensively collect detailed data about their Internet market, as well as obtain precise measures of which pages in their sites were visited, for how long, how the individuals came to the site, and where the visitors originated. The Internet also has the capabilities to gather consumer reactions to current products and ads as well as product and ad concepts through such means as online focus groups.

Global Exposure. The Internet also reaches a worldwide audience. Clearly, the Internet expands the company's market to include global markets, allowing those from around the world to visit the web site. Companies can respond to this global accessibility easily by having pages available in languages other than English. Gaining brand recognition from a global market could give a company the competitive advantage it needs in a marketplace that is increasingly expanding its borders.

Customization. The Internet's interactive nature allows for greater flexibility than traditional media in type of information transmitted and the method of transmission. For instance, decisions regarding whether the information should be technically advanced or simple, whether the information should be textual, graphic, video or auditory, and whether a product demonstration or detailed product description is used, can all be made by the consumer rather than the advertiser.

Enhance Customer-Company Relations. Internet advertisements can also be used as a customer service vehicle. For instance, relationships can be enhanced through being available upon demand all day, every day , reducing purchase uncertainty through online product trials or demonstrations , and providing online, up-to-date, accurate technical support .

Role Playing. Another important feature of the Internet is its capabilities in creating a more persuasive and engaging ad. Through the use of interactive games and contests, the online site can encourage role-playing . Through role-playing, the consumer generates arguments in favor of the product , which is often more persuasive to the individual than other-generated arguments .

Purchase Facilitation. Finally, the Internet can facilitate purchase decisions not only by providing detailed product and purchase details (e.g., by finding the nearest dealer and quoting prices), but also by giving consumers the option of buying at that moment from their own homes. This removes the gap between ad exposure and purchase response , creating the opportunity for the ultimate in impulse buying.

In this chapter, we examine whether current commercial sites are incorporating features that allow the companies to achieve the nine potential benefits outlined previously: providing detailed product information; supplying accurate, up-to-date information; building and fostering brand image; collecting information about their on-line customers; reaching and enhancing relationships with a global market; allowing customers to tailor the advertising experience to meet their own needs; enhancing customer-company relations by providing accurate, personalized customer service; engaging customers in role-playing; and facilitating purchase decisions.

The Incorporation of Online Advertisements with Print Advertising

In the midst of all of these potential benefits of online advertising, there is the challenge of attracting visitors to one's site. One solution is to advertise the site online by renting space on a site or purchasing keyword-search space. However, relying on this approach alone, poses several problems, one of which is that the audience is limited to those already on the Internet. In addition, it is unlikely that the online ad will reach all potentially interested Internet users; hence, there will be those who remain unaware of the site.

Another, more compelling solution to attracting consumers to the site is to promote a site through the use of traditional media. Print media is particularly useful because the interested consumer can directly refer to the print advertisement when typing the Uniform Resource Locator (URL). This reduces the likelihood of errors due to hastily copying on paper or memorizing the URL from a television, radio, or billboard advertisement. Recent evidence suggests that the use of one mixed-media strategy (promoting a web site in magazine ads) has increased at a nearly exponential rate .*PC Computing* in November, 1994, and that just over one year later, 50% of all the ads in *PC Computing* contained a URL, with similar growth rates in the other publications. In addition, preliminary research suggests that using magazines to locate sites on the Internet is far from uncommon; 65% of respondents reported finding out about web sites through magazines.

The way in which advertisers incorporate the online site and the print ad varies, however. For instance, many advertised URLs take the consumer to the homepage, which may or may not directly link to the product advertised in the print ad. The prominence and context of the URL in the print ad, the degree to which the print ad attempts to persuade consumers to visit the web site, and the amount of information describing the web site also varies considerably.

TABLE 8-1: Comparison of the Presence of URLs

Magazine	*Date of First URL*	*Percentage of Print Ads With URLs in Jan., 1996*
PC Computing	November 1994	50%
Newsweek	April 1995	32%
Money	May 1995	28%
Glamour	September 1995	10%

Research Questions

In this research, we focus on the mixed-media strategy of advertising online and publicizing the online exhibit in a magazine ad. Our two primary objectives are to (1) assess the degree to which online advertisers are currently taking advantage of the potential benefits of advertising on the Internet as outlined previously, and (2) assess the degree to which web sites and print ads are integrated.

Methodology

Selection of Ads

From a list of magazine categories used in prior market research studies , categories were selected to provide a broad range of the magazine markets which varied in technical knowledge, sex, and age. Among those selected are business, news, beauty/fashion, entertainment, youth, and food/home magazines. Within these categories, the magazines with the highest circulation statistics according to the most recent *World Almanac* (1995) were chosen as the source of print advertisements included in the study sample.. The magazines selected were *Business Week, Newsweek, Glamour, Rolling Stone, Seventeen,* and *Better Homes and Gardens.* Only the most recent issue at the time of coding was evaluated. Those advertisements less than one sixth of a page or in the classifieds section were excluded. Of the remaining print ads, those listing a URL referring to a site on the World Wide Web were analyzed along with their web sites.

Measurement

Features Capturing the Nine Benefits of Advertising Online

To benefit from a web site, the advertiser must include features that would allow the site to yield that benefit. For instance, one cannot expect a company to benefit from the global accessibility of the Internet if the site does not contain such content as currency information, international shipping fees, and product availability for countries outside the manufacturer's. Thus, to measure the degree to which a commercial web site is utilizing the Internet in ways to attain the potential benefits, four features per benefit were identified that would help in attaining that benefit. These features were specific to an identified benefit, many of which were provided in the literature as examples of the potential benefit. Care was taken to ensure that each feature was independent from the other features within and across benefits. Each feature was coded dichotomously as either present (1) or absent (0) in the web site. For each advertised web site, a score between 0 and 4 was obtained for each potential benefit by aggregating across the four features for the benefit.

The following are the nine benefits, each with an example feature: (1) provides content rich information (e.g., do they elaborate upon product/service features or provide detailed performance data?); (2) updates information and informs their visitors of updates (e.g., do they have a "what's new" or "what's coming" section?); (3) builds brand image (e.g., do they have links to other interesting sites or have trivia about the company and its product?); (4) employs data collection methods (e.g., do they request feedback about the web site or existing products?); (5) responds to the potentially global market (e.g., do they have pages about their product or their company translated into other languages?; (6) gives consumers the option of customizing the information (e.g., do they have the information at various levels of technicality, available in graphical, textual, auditory, and/or video form?); (7) attempts to enhance customer-company relations (e.g., do they provide an e-mail address for consumer questions/comments or have an online discussion page?); (8) encourages role-playing (e.g., do they have interactive games or product simulations?); and (9) facilitates purchase intentions (e.g., do they offer multiple purchasing methods including online methods?).

Additional questions were asked to learn more details about current online advertising practices. For example, the judges coding the sites indicated the ease of finding certain items (e.g., whether such features as a "what's new" section were listed on the initial page or homepage), how frequently time sensitive items (e.g., press releases, prices, product availability) were updated, which data collection methods and incentives were most commonly used, how technically advanced the sites were, and whether the sites were using recommended methods for tying offline sales to the web site (e. g, by providing "computer coupons").

Including all features for each benefit would result in an overwhelming amount of information for the consumer to sift through without good navigational tools. Many web style guides mention the importance of including navigational tools such as a search engine. To investigate the advertised sites' use of navigational tools, we identified four tools and coded the site as either having each navigational tool (1) or not (0). The ease of finding these tools (e.g., whether they are located on every page) was also assessed. To receive information regarding the coding items for the nine benefits and the navigational tools, please contact the authors.

In addition to these objective measures of the site, there was one subjective measure: whether the judge liked the site. This measure was added after all of the coding was completed to capture the judge's overall impression of the web site. This was coded dichotomously: The judge either liked the site (1) or did not (0).

Because the inclusion of a feature might vary by product type, the judges recorded the product advertised in the print ad. When more than one product was advertised, the product featured prominently in the ad was selected. If all of the products were similarly displayed, one of the products was randomly selected. The products advertised in the print ads were later categorized as technically advanced (i.e., requiring more technical information such as cars, computer equipment, financial products; these are often products that require a large monetary investment, thereby motivating consumers to seek detailed information) or technically simple (requiring less technical information such as food, beverages, and clothing; these are often products that require a relatively small monetary investment).

Integration of Web Site and Print Advertisement

To examine the integration of the web site and the print ad, we noted the size and placement of the URL in the print ad, whether the ad made specific reference to the URL, and whether the advertised product could be easily located on the web site. We also compared the web site's and print ad's number of product visuals and the amount of product information.

Sample

There were 5 to 24 print advertisements with URLs in each magazine (excluding those less than one sixth of a page or in the classifieds section), with the most appearing in *Business Week* (n = 24; 50% of total ads in that magazine) and the fewest in *Seventeen* (n = 5; 6% of the ads in that magazine). There were a total of 65 distinct ads listing URLs, with 95% of the ads covering a full page or more.

TABLE 8-2: URLs Present in Magazines Sampled

Magazine	*Number of Ads with URLs*	*Percentage of Ads with URLs*
Business Week	24	50%
Newsweek	12	35%
Rolling Stone	22	30%
Better Homes and Gardens	13	10%
Glamour	9	6%
Seventeen	5	6%
TOTAL	85 total ads, 65 distinct ads	17%

Of the 65 print ads 10 displayed multiple products. All of the advertised products within a print ad were from the same product category (e.g., computer software, cosmetics), and therefore random selection of one of the products did not influence the type of product examined (i.e., whether it was technically advanced or simple).

The features capturing the nine potential benefits of a web site, additional details of the web site, navigational ease, the subjective measure, product type, and the integration of the web site with the print ad were examined for each of the 65 ads.

Results

Making Use of the Benefits of a Commercial Web Site

To assess the degree to which the 65 advertised web sites incorporated features that would help them attain the nine benefits, the number of features present were summed for each benefit such that the highest score possible was 4 (incorporates four features for that benefit) and the lowest score possible was 0 (incorporates no features for that benefit). The scores averaged across all 65 sites indicate that, overall, the sites included approximately half or fewer of the features for each benefit ($M = 1.65$ across all sites and benefits; only two of the nine benefits had average scores above 2, indicating that on average, sites included more than half of the features for that benefit).

On average, the web sites included more of the features to take advantage of the content richness of the medium and the ability to build brand image. Most sites used the content richness of the medium to elaborate on product features (75% of all sites). Fewer displayed their products with more than one visual (46%). In terms of building brand image, most sites had details about sponsored events (62%) and linked to interesting sites outside their web site (59%). Fewer sites, however, attempted to build brand image through the use of customer testimonials (31%). Furthermore, most sites virtually ignored those features addressing the global accessibility of the medium and its role playing capabilities.

One might argue that having multiple features for each benefit is unnecessary and that having at least one feature is sufficient for the company to attain that benefit. Although most of the sites included at least one feature from six or more of the nine benefits, only 12% of the sites incorporated into their web site at least one feature from each of the nine benefits.

TABLE 8-3: Mean Benefit Scores

Benefits	*Mean*	*(SD)*
1. Content-Rich Information	2.32	(1.39)
2. Ease of Updating	1.18	(0.98)
3. Build Brand Image	2.51	(1.00)
4. Collect Detailed Data	2.11	(1.20)
5. Global Accessibility	0.74	(1.11)
6. Customized Advertisement	1.91	(0.98)
7. Enhance Company-Customer Relations	1.66	(1.11)
8. Role-Playing	0.69	(0.80)
9. Facilitate Purchase Intention	1.72	(1.24)
10. Navigational Tools	2.26	(1.16)

Furthermore, although all of the sites incorporated at least one feature to build brand image, the majority of sites failed to include at least one feature to attain the benefits of the global nature and the role-playing capabilities of the medium. In addition, nearly one quarter of the sites failed to have at least one feature taking advantage of the ease of updating the information and facilitating purchase intentions. This included such features as notifying visitors of upcoming changes to the site and locating the nearest store or dealer, neither of which are difficult features to incorporate into a site, although they do require an ongoing commitment to keeping the site current.

Although for most of the nine benefits, 75% or more of the sites included at least one of the four identified features, it is questionable whether a single feature alone can attain the benefit. For instance, looking more specifically at the features incorporated into the site for the ease of updating, we find that nearly half of the sites mentioned when the site was last updated (44%) and what was new at the site (48%), but few mentioned whether they regularly update the site or announced upcoming features of the site. In addition, although the Internet allows for the gathering of detailed customer information, most sites collected demographic and customer contact information (51% or more), with fewer gathering reactions to web sites or to products (less than 35%). Most sites enhanced communication with the company (thereby enhancing company-customer relations) through the availability of the company's e-mail address (68%). Few enhanced relations, however, through more novel methods such as adding the customer to a newsgroup or list server (35%) or having a discussion page (20%). These novel features would allow the company to share more information with the consumer and build brand image as their ongoing relations with customers are displayed. This technique would also provide more information about their online consumers.

TABLE 8-4: Cumulative Benefits

Number of Benefits with at Least One Feature	*Percentage of 65*	*Cumulative*
0	0%	0%
1	2%	2%
2	0%	2%
3	0%	2%
4	3%	5%
5	5%	10%
6	26%	36%
7	20%	56%
8	32%	88%
9	12%	100%

Perhaps most surprising is that the sites made little use of the interactive nature of the medium. For instance, most products were presented textually (94%) and/or graphically (77%) with few being presented auditorially or as video (less than 20%). In addition, only a few sites offered information at various levels of technicality (44% or less), and had such technically advanced features as words running across the bottom of the screen (14%) or frames (6%).

These advanced features can be useful in guiding the consumer to particular pages within the site. For instance, words running across the bottom of the screen can be used to attract attention to a particular feature of the web site. In addition, frames can be used as a navigational device by having them serve as a table of contents alongside the main text.

Furthermore, only a few sites encouraged impulse buying on the Internet by taking online orders (18%). This finding is especially important in light of how many businesses express disappointment with online sales. Only 43% of these sites located the nearest store or dealer, and few mentioned such details as their return policy (14%) and their product availability (11%). What is more, few made attempts to tie offline purchases to the web site through an order form that could be faxed/mailed (20%). Only 2% provided coupons via the Internet that could be redeemed online or offline.

The currency of the time-dependent information appears to depend greatly upon the type of information being updated. For instance, of the sites listing prices, only 18% had updated the prices within the last month. The "press release" pages, however, were kept much more current. The vast majority (73%) of those having such a page updated it within the last month. This result may be due to prices not changing as often as new press releases are generated. Furthermore, once press releases are created, they can easily and inexpensively be put on a web site along with a date.

TABLE 8-5: Features Incorporated by Benefit

	Number of Features Incorporated				
Benefits	***0***	***1***	***2***	***3***	***4***
Content Rich Information	11%	25%	14%	23%	28%
Ease of Updating	25%	45%	22%	6%	3%
Build Brand Image	0%	20%	26%	37%	17%
Collect Detailed Data	11%	20%	31%	25%	14%
Global Accessibility	59%	25%	5%	9%	3%
Customized Advertisement	5%	31%	42%	15%	8%
Enhance Company-Customer Relations	14%	35%	28%	17%	6 %
Role-Playing	51%	31%	17%	2%	0%
Facilitate Purchase Intention	23%	19%	28%	25%	6%
Navigational Tools	8%	19%	29%	29%	15%

By including the features of many of these benefits, the online site can become quite complex, thereby requiring the accessibility of navigational tools.

Overall, the sites made use of approximately half of the navigational features under investigation ($M = 2.26$, see Table 8.3). Most sites had home and section icons on each page (69%), but few had an overview of the site (31%). Moreover, although web style guides agree on the primary importance of a search engine, less than half of the sites had one to assist consumers in navigating through a site (34%). Of those with a search engine or an outline of the site, only approximately half (59% and 55%, respectively) of the sites had the feature located on every page. If these features are not accessible from every page in the site, then the consumer must learn how the site is organized in order to recall where such navigational tools are and are not available.

It appears that many commercial sites lack the features that would allow the company to benefit from having an exhibit on the Internet. Most of the included features increase the volume of information, but few made use of the interactive, global features of the medium. Moreover, although the sites were complex and content-rich, most commercial sites failed to include many of the navigational tools necessary to assist visitors in finding their way around the site.

Navigational tools, however, appear to be an especially important feature of a site. The only feature significantly related to liking the site was the availability of navigational tools ($r = .42$, p.001). This suggests that regardless of how much information is available from a site, how many interesting bits of trivia are included, how many visuals, contests, games, or online discussions are present, visitors will have a favorable impression only if multiple navigational tools are available.

To examine the relationship among the benefits, we applied a principal factor analysis to the ad by benefit (65 x 9) matrix. The first three factors have eight values greater than 1 and together explain 53% of the variance. Additional factors each explain less than 10% of the variance. After applying a Varimax rotation, the following factor pattern was indicated (only those items with values greater than .40 are included within a factor).

The first factor appears to capture the interactive nature of the medium, thereby allowing the consumer to be an active participant. This first factor, which accounts for more of the variance than the other two factors, includes the benefits of letting the consumer customize the advertisement, encouraging role playing, and having multiple navigational tools available so the consumer can navigate easily around the site. The second factor appears to capture the company's commitment to having an ongoing, online communication with consumers. That is, they offer up-to-date information, they collect detailed information about the consumer, and they include features to enhance company customer relations - all of which require significant human labor. The third factor appears to capture attempts to enhance sales by providing both sales and brand-image information. This factor includes providing detailed product and brand information, providing such information for other countries, and providing purchase-related information. Hence, there appear to be three components to current Internet advertising strategies: site interactivity, communication with the company, and traditional sales-based content. Although the first component, interactivity, is the most discriminating among the online ads, the benefits characteristic of the third component, traditional sales approaches, is most common among online advertisers.

Finally, the examination of product types reveals that sites with technically advanced products incorporated more features of each benefit than those sites with technically simple products.

This is especially the case for the inclusion of rich product information, updates, brand information, and navigational tools. In terms of information richness, more sites marketing technically advanced than technically simple products elaborated on product features (84% vs. 67%, $x^2(1, 65) = 2.75, p = .098$), provided detailed performance data (66% vs. 39%, $x^2(1, 65) = 4.48, p$ .05). described multiple products (75% vs. 42%, $x^2(1, 65) = 7.10$, p 01), and had multiple visuals of the same product (59% vs. 33%,x^2 65) = 4.43, p .05).

In terms of keeping the information updated, more sites marketing technically advanced than technically simple products had a "what's new" section (66% vs. 33% respectively, $x^2(1, 65) = 5.54, p .05$), a "what's coming" section (22% vs. 6%, $x^2(1, 65) = 3.41, p$

= .065), a "press release" section (72% vs. 39%, $x^2(1, 65) = 7.47$, $p < .05$), and mentioned how often the site was updated (22% vs. 3 %, $x^2(1, 65) = 5.35$, $p < .05$).

TABLE 8-6: Benefit Factor Structure

Benefits	*Factor 1*	*Factor 2*	*Factor 3*
Content Rich Information			.73
Ease of Updating		.79	
Build Brand Image			.69
Collect Detailed Data		.57	
Global Accessibility			.55
Customized Advertisement	.84		
Enhance Company-Customer Relations		.67	
Role-Playing	.54		
Facilitate Purchase Intention			.50
Navigational Tools	.72		

Regarding the inclusion of brand information, the only feature included more by sites promoting technically advanced rather than technically simple products was the inclusion of details about sponsored events or other supported causes (81% vs. 42%, $x^2(1, 65) = 10.35$, $p < .001$).

In examining the inclusion of navigational tools, those sites with technically advanced products were more likely to have a search engine than were those sites with technically simple products (50% vs. 27% respectively, $x^2(1, 65) = 7.35$, $p < .01$), and were somewhat more likely to have an outline of the site (41% vs. 21%, $x^2(1, 65) = 2.87$, $p = .09$).

Although the average number of features allowing customers to customize sites was no higher for sites with technically advanced products as opposed to technically simple products, the sites with technically advanced products were more likely to have information available at various levels of technicality (53% vs 15%, x2(1, 65) = 10.46, p <.001). In addition, more sites with technically advanced products provided price information than did sites with technically simple products (63% vs. 36%, $x^2(1, 65) = 4.44$, $p < .05$). This last finding may be due to the larger monetary investment (and, hence, consumers' greater concern with pricing) for products that are technically advanced versus simple.

TABLE 8-7: Benefits by Product Types

Benefits	*Technically Advanced*	*Technically Simple*	*(63)*
Content Rich Information	2.84	1.82	3.17*
Ease of Updating	1.59	.79	3.60*
Build Brand Image	2.81	2.21	2.51
Collect Detailed Data	2.28	1.94	1.15
Global Accessibility	.97	.51	1.66
Customized Advertisement	2.00	1.82	.75
Enhance Company-Customer Relations	1.69	1.64	.19
Role-Playing	.75	.64	.56
Facilitate Purchase Intention	1.88	1.58	.97
Navigational Tools	2.63	1.91	2.59*

*$p < .05$

Incorporation of Mixed-Media Advertising Strategies

In addition to examining whether online commercial sites are incorporating features that would allow them to benefit from being on the Internet, we also examined the use of print media in guiding a consumer toward a site and toward a specific product or service.

We found that although a growing number of magazine ads included URLs, it appears that the URL still played a minor part in the print ad. For instance, the URL was often listed in small print, near the copyright information (40%). Only a few advertised the web site (5%) rather than the company or a product. Furthermore, few advertisements guided the consumer directly to the online product information. For 59% of the sites, it was difficult to find the advertised product on the web site. That is, there was no immediate reference to the product advertised in print on the first page to which the advertised URL linked. In fact, for 9% of the sites, the product advertised in the print ad could not be found anywhere on the web site. In contrast, within its print ad, Kodak guided the consumer directly to online information of the advertised product. Although their URL, , was in small print near the copyright information, it instructed the consumer to click on "What's Hot" and then "Serious Fun," which led the consumer directly to information on the advertised camera and additional product-related information.

Overall, the web sites contained more information about the advertised product than the print ad did ($M = 1.53$). Not surprisingly, this was especially true for the technically advanced products ($M = 1.72$) than for the technically simple products ($M = 1.33$, $t(63) = 2.19$, $p < .05$). That is, due to the complexity of the technically advanced versus the technically simple products, it is more likely that such products as computers would have significantly more information in the web exhibit than the print ad, whereas such products as tweezers and shoes would have only slightly more information in the web exhibit than in the print ad.

Advertising one's web site in other media may be a viable solution for attracting people to a site. However few advertisements directed the consumer's attention to the URL, much less listed the benefits of visiting the site. Moreover, even fewer advertisements guided the consumer directly to the web page where the product was described, often leaving the consumer to hunt for the product. This can often be quite an endeavor without the presence of such navigational tools as a search engine or outline. Hence, although more information is included in online ads than in print ads, there does not yet appear to be effective integration of print and online advertising.

Conclusions and Discussion

Benefits of Online Advertising

The results suggest that on average, commercial web sites incorporate approximately half or fewer of the identified beneficial features of advertising on the Web. Most web sites are taking advantage of the content richness of the medium and the ability to build brand image while ignoring the benefits attainable through its global accessibility and role-playing capabilities. It appears that commercial web sites include many of the features that traditional media are capable of handling (e.g., listing product descriptions and specifications textually and graphically, listing information about the company and upcoming sponsored events). However, most sites do not include many of the features unique to the Internet (e.g., online discussions, the choice of textual, graphical, auditory, and video product descriptions, interactive games, product simulations, online purchase orders). Indeed, the factor analysis results suggest that current online advertising can be described in terms of a three-pronged approach involving interactivity, customer-company communication, and traditional content. Commercial web sites appear to concentrate on this third factor. Taken together, these findings suggest that online businesses may be transplanting their marketing strategies from other media to the Internet, thereby missing many of the beneficial possibilities offered by the interactive, time- and space-independent features of the Internet.

Although most of the sites did include at least one feature from six or more of the nine benefits, many of the commonly included features were static broadcast messages (e.g., product specifications) rather than interactive (e.g., interactive contests). In addition, many of these features increased the volume of information, thereby increasing the complexity of the web site. The potential benefits attainable from these features may not be realized if the resulting volume of information overwhelms the consumer.

One way to avoid overloading the consumer with information is to provide navigational tools. Indeed, the results of this study indicate that navigational tools are an especially important feature of a site: The more tools available at the commercial web site, the better it was liked. The results also suggest that commercial web sites include navigational tools that allow the consumer to move easily between pages (e.g., by having home and section icons on every page), but lack those tools that would assist consumers in information acquisition (e.g., by having a search engine or some outline or overview of the site). These latter tools are those argued to be necessary features of a site, especially a complex one.

It is possible, however, that some of the beneficial features identified might be more applicable to certain types of products than others. We explored this possibility in terms of how technically complex the advertised product was. We found that in comparison with those sites promoting technically simple products, sites promoting technically advanced products incorporated more features using the content richness of the medium, the ease of updating, and the ability to build brand image. Furthermore, the sites marketing technically advanced products included more navigational tools than did those marketing technically simple products. It is possible that sites exhibiting such technically advanced products as computers and cars have more product information, have information that changes more frequently, and are more likely to have such image-related information as trade shows and sponsored events, than sites exhibiting such technically simple products as lip gloss and beverages. As a result of having more information overall, the importance of navigational tools might be especially salient to the design of web sites promoting technically advanced products. Even though sites marketing technically advanced products currently include more of the beneficial features than the sites marketing technically simple products, a future empirical question is whether sites with technically advanced products benefit more by including these features in their sites than those with technically simple products would.

Although our study does not directly assess whether incorporating the beneficial features into a site leads to a successful site (indeed, this would be difficult to assess given the lack of agreement in the field over the appropriate benchmark to use in identifying web site success), one can imagine the likely consequences of ignoring many of the unique features of the Internet. For instance, because all sites on the Internet are globally accessible, a site that ignores its global audience might turn away potential customers who identify the site as applicable only to certain regions. Such an identification might be difficult to later counteract. Moreover, ignoring such interactive features of the Internet as its role-playing capabilities and its ability to enhance company customer communication may lose the majority of the Internet audience who are less interested in sites infected with "brochure ware" or "brochuritis". Such sites are unlikely to encourage repeat visits. Experimentally manipulating the presence of such features as interactivity and communicability within the same site to assess their effects on web site experiences and evaluations would be a worthwhile future research endeavor.

Mixed-Media Advertising Strategy

Surprisingly, although many advertisements included a URL in the print advertisement, few actively promoted the site in the print ads. That is, most of the URLs were listed on the periphery of the print ad, without any specific reference to the specialized features of the web site. Moreover, although the sites contained detailed information beyond what was available in the print ad, for the majority of advertised web sites, locating the product within the web site was difficult. In fact, some of the products advertised in the print ads could not be found anywhere in the web site. If the print ad is successful in stimulating interest in the advertised product, then listing a URL that links directly to a web page without reference to the advertised product defeats the purpose of listing the URL in the print ad, as well as defeats the purpose of having detailed product information in the web site beyond what is available in the print ad.

This is particularly true when navigational tools such as a search engine are absent.

Why are Online Companies Disillusioned? Some Preliminary Answers

It is possible that companies are disillusioned with advertising on the Internet because their strategies preclude them from the benefits attainable through having a web site. In the sample of commercial sites examined here, the sites did not include many of the features allowing them to benefit from having a web site. Moreover, they had few navigational tools, making it difficult for visitors to realize all of the features of the site. Although these businesses employed a mixed-media advertising strategy by advertising their URL in another medium, few actively promoted the site and its features. In addition, the products advertised in print were often difficult to find online.

It appears that many of these weaknesses are caused by applying traditional advertising strategies to a dynamic environment, hence ignoring the unique features possible through the interactive nature of the medium. One example from this research is the failure to allow customers to customize the information (e.g., by including information at various levels of technicality). There is no need for the online advertisement to streamline the information for only one type of customer. Because the Internet has no limits in the amount of information provided in an online commercial exhibit, the web site can provide information to meet the majority of consumers' needs and interests. In addition, given the interactive nature of the medium, the web site can tailor the information for each consumer's needs (e.g., by providing an online form asking consumers what information they are looking for and how they would like the information presented). or consumers can select the information suiting their own needs (e.g., by selecting information that is designed for a younger or older market, toward those interested in testimonials versus product specifications, toward those willing versus unwilling to wait for elaborate graphics to download).

In addition, by transplanting traditional marketing strategies to a web site, one also ignores the unique problems posed by the Internet. Examples of problems specific to the Internet include encouraging people to visit the site and encouraging those who visit to return. One method of encouraging people to visit a site is by listing the site's URL in a print ad. Yet, listing the company's URL as if it were an 800-number or address is likely ineffective. The unique features of the site should be highlighted within the ad. For instance, food distributors could entice consumers to visit their web site by advertising in print that the site contains recipes for various events (e.g., the Super Bowl) and diets. Without such enticements, consumers may have little motivation to visit the site. This will likely become especially true as more companies go online, thereby reducing the novelty of merely having a web site. Moreover, as this study suggests, listing only the URL is ineffective in guiding the consumer to online product information. An inability to find the online product information will likely dissuade rather than persuade the consumer to purchase the product (and revisit the site).

Recommended methods of encouraging repeat visits include making the site interactive and updating the site frequently. Both of these interactive features are unique to the Internet, and as this study suggests, are largely ignored by online advertisers. Hence, although current commercial sites appear to be making the site informative (e.g., by providing detailed product descriptions), this is likely insufficient to encourage repeat visits; the site will need to be entertaining as well (e.g., by having such interactive features as online discussions and product simulations).

In creating an online commercial site, it is important to recognize that the Internet requires different marketing and advertising practices than those used in traditional media and that mixed-media advertising requires coordinated efforts between those designing the web site and those designing advertisements for other media.

9

LEARNING OF WORLD WIDE WEB

There are three reasons that research on college students attitudes toward learning on the World Wide Web (WWW) is important. Instructional and user interface designers (UI) need data on novice Web users, particularly learners in the domain of education, to build more user-friendly browser interfaces. Web browser designers who are creating new features and enhancing existing features for online services also need this research to understand how to make browsers more intuitive. Novices' attitudes toward computer learning affect their performance; as textbooks are replaced by computers as teaching delivery mechanisms, authors and publishers must consider how attitudes affect comprehension.

In this chapter, I profile novice Web users and describe characteristics unique to this target population, characteristics based on their attitudes and their performance when completing typical scenarios using the Netscape browser. Because of their inexperience and overconfidence, novices accessing curriculum via the WWW face impediments in using a browser efficiently and show decreased levels of comprehension. A list of implications offers ways to ease the learning curve for novice Web users exposed to Web technology at college levels.

To pinpoint attitudinal differences between novices and expert Web users, I conducted a study that analyzed three scores: usability, attitude, and comprehension. Two scores, browser usability and Web attitude, are discussed in this chapter. Participants were considered novices if they had never used the WWW; they were considered experienced if they had used the WWW at least two times. The usability score measured how many scenarios testers successfully completed and rated whether navigation and control over the display were easy and intuitive. The attitude score evaluated the testers' receptivity to incorporating Web technology into their university programs.

I used the Web Attitude Measure (WAM) to determine how receptive college learners were to using the WWW for curriculum delivery and comprehension testing. The hour-long session consisted of a sequence of tasks: signing a consent form, completing five scenarios using the browser, receiving instruction on the five scenarios, completing the WAM, reading curriculum on the WWW, closing the network connection, and finally, answering questions on the curriculum. No tasks had time limits, to encourage novice users to experiment and explore the browser functionality without pressure. The results indicated that previous experience using the Netscape browser significantly increased usability, attitude, and comprehension.

Novice Web User Demographics

Ninety-seven University of New Mexico (UNM) undergraduate and postgraduate students participated in the study; novice Web users predominated because I had advertised for people with no or little Web experience. Only 32 of the 65 subjects had ever used the WWW before the research session. The baseline requirements to participate were a minimum age of 17 years, enrollment at UNM, computer keyboard skills, and 1 hour for testing. Subjects filled out a questionnaire with demographic data to distinguish those with experience in computers and E-mail from those with Web experience. There was a nearly even distribution by gender and age, with 52 subjects under 25 and 41. The amount of computer and E-mail experience among novice Web users confirmed that novice Web users are computer and E-mail literate and that distinct skills are required for Web literacy.

To establish usage patterns, experts were asked specific questions about the amounts of time they spent on the WWW weekly and what Web sites they visited. Out of 32 experts, nineteen previously used the Netscape browser, fourteen logged on from school, and sixteen browsed articles, references, papers, and weather sites. Many respondents commented that they "surf" and "browse" for "entertainment" and "crafts" as they looked for Web pages relating to their hobbies or recreational interests.

Novice Web Users Speak Out on Browser Usability

To evaluate the performance usability of the Netscape browser (version 1.1), I asked participants to perform certain tasks considered typical for the WWW. The test session started with the browser open to the UNM home page. Participants then tested five different browser interface features that followed a logical sequence from simple to more difficult. After each scenario, participants

TABLE 9-1: Demographic Analysis of Sample

	Gender	*Computer Usage*	*E-mail Usage*	*Avg Hours Browse Web (Per Session)*
Novice	M 21	Under 1 yr 15	Daily 7	
	F 44	1 - 3 yrs 25	Weekly 30	
		4 - 6 yrs 15	Monthly 3	
		7 + yrs 10	Rarely 25	
Experienced	M 14	Under 1 yr 4	Daily 13	Under 1 hr 20
	F 18	1 - 3 yrs 7	Weekly 15	1 - 2 hrs 9
	4-6	yrs 8	Monthly 0	3 + hrs 3
		7 + yrs 13	Rarely 4	

Among all the testers, the *perception* of usability was very high $F(2, 93) = 12$, but the actual *performance* was low. This dichotomy between user perception and performance clearly illustrates that users are unaware of their usability problems with the browser interface. Novice and expert users had nearly identical mean perceived usability scores; the average score was 4.4 out of a total possible score of 5. Actual usability scores revealed this discrepancy between perceived usability and actual performance, as indicated in the responses to the five scenarios.

TABLE 9-2: Actual Usability Scenarios Correct (%) by Novice and Experienced Users

Usability Scenarios	*Novice (67%)*	*Exp (33%)*
Scenario 1: Go to the Libraries page.	75%	88%
Scenario 2: Return to the previous page.	57%	84%
Scenario 3: Go to the University of New Mexico Web page.	63%	84%
What is the Web address?	57%	88%
Scenario 4: Change the display font to Large.	11%	38%
Scenario 5: Look for Web sites relating to Psychology.	37%	60%

Testers were first asked to connect to a Web page, then to return to the previous page, then to find the UNM home page address or uniform resource locator (URL), then to change the font size, and finally to complete a search for other Web sites relating to education or psychology. Novices performed poorly on these tasks because of the usability of the browser. The percentage of successfully completed scenarios was consistently lower for novice users compared to experienced users. Dramatically low completion rates were tabulated even for experienced users for the two more difficult scenarios. These low usability scores indicate that both advanced navigation and browser display control features cause confusion for users. User questions and comments were collected during and after the scenarios by using a checklist to record behavior patterns in relation to browser usability. Preference settings to change the display fonts are one instance of browser design incongruous with users' cognitive models.

All participants had trouble changing the font size and finding preferences off the main menu bar. Both novice and expert users erroneously looked for menu bar labels consistent with word-processing software categories, like Edit or Format, to change the browser text font. This fact was indicated by user comments recorded during the usability trials: "I'm looking for the format option to change the font size," "Where is the Edit choice to get to fonts?" The general preferences menu category and font option were illogically grouped with other types of browser application settings and hidden three levels deep. Novices and experts could not complete the task because they did not make the distinction between the page display and the browser settings. It was clear from the comments and questions that browser usability was not intuitive for other reasons as well. Even when testers successfully completed the scenario, it was not obvious to them why the text font size changed and the image map font did not; users did not understand that font in an image map is part of the graphic. There was also confusion between local network and Internet connections. On the basis of responses to the last scenario, there was conclusive evidence that participants did not make a distinction between a search on the local university Web page and one on the Web. Nearly all the users who thought they had completed an internet search, had actually written a Web address local to the university as a response. Few of the users, novice or expert, actually found the browser search icon or any of the Internet search engines. While the participants were completing the scenarios, I observed them, and completed a checklist of their behaviors and the mechanical problems that might have affected their completion rate. I also recorded participants' specific questions for analysis. Most problems observed were mechanical: The mouse failed, the Internet connection broke, an Insufficient Memory message appeared. Typically, when these problems arose, the person was moved to another machine to continue the trials without delay. Non-mechanical difficulties were due to students' unfamiliarity with the interface. At every interaction, subjects were reminded that the purpose of the scenarios was to test the performance usability of the browser, Netscape; if they could not complete a trial, they were to write down what they had tried and then move on to the next trial. I continually reassured the testers that any difficulties in completing the scenarios meant that the browser design needed to be refined and improved to be more intuitive. Despite my message, many testers wasted time on the third and fourth scenarios and never tried the fifth and hardest scenario. The most typical questions students asked pointed to the key problems with the interface and the WWW. These included:

- How do I go to the main menu?
- How do I find fonts? I'm looking for Options on the menu.
- What do I do if I can't answer questions?
- Is Netscape considered a browser?
- What do you mean by *navigate?* Am I on the last page? What happens when I get stuck on a screen and can't get back?
- I can't find the home page. Is this screen considered a Web page? I don't know where to find a Web page.
- (*Closes Netscape*) "I'm not sure how I did that."
- (*Clicks icon*) "Is it that simple?"
- (*Clicks bullet, not hyperlink*) How do I go to the next page?

Even after instruction on how to complete all the scenarios, novice users found it difficult to access the curriculum. The destination address at the bottom corner of the browser window was too subtle a cue that different links navigated to other local or Internet pages. The jargon used in the scenario questions and on the browser interface, such as browser, Web, home page, hyperlink, and Web address, impeded usability and prevented users from focusing on the task at hand.

Novice Web User Issues for Interface Design

Novice users rarely distinguish between the browser interface and the document; therefore, they are usually perplexed when the two behave differently. Nabkel and Shafir explained that "the boundary between application interfaces and their interactive content has blurred and continues to disintegrate." Unlike word-processing or desktop-publishing software, browser interfaces do not allow designers to control font style and size, alignment, window size, and other aspects of document design.

The fact that browser interface design affects users' cognition, behavior, and attitude presents many challenges to browser interface designers. The overwhelming interest in the Internet and the multi-platform environment in which it exists generate a wide variety of screen design and display problems. Monitor screens lack any spatial cues, and computer-based instruction has no physical properties, like page numbers in a paper textbook. Without page numbers and chapter layout divisions to assist in dividing information, informational grouping on screen does not fall into discrete display units. Visually, text, graphics, and the way the browser interface window displays them are intricately interwoven. Continued research in human factors would help meet these design challenges and facilitate novice Web users' learning via the WWW. Composing information in a browser interface also poses complex problems affecting novice user attitudes.

Novice Web User Attitudes

The Web Attitude Measure (WAM) is an instrument based on Kay's (1989) Computer Attitude Measure (CAM), that was modified to focus specifically on the WWW, rather than on computers in general. The WAM is divided into four sub-scales: behavior, affect, attitude, adjective. The relation between usability and the attitude sub-scale illuminates interesting points about novice Web users. When a one-way Analysis of Variance was performed on affective scores by web experience, there is a significant difference by experience $F(2,94)=14.9622$. Every question in the affective sub-scale, confirms a significant effect on affective scores for experienced users.

TABLE 9.3: Standard Deviation and Effect on Affective Scores for Experienced Users

Affective Questions	*SD*	*F*
I feel I need an experienced person nearby when I use the WWW.	1.909	.000
I need someone to tell me the best way to use the WWW.	1.738	.000
I could probably teach myself most of the things I need to know about the WWW.	1.846	.000
I can make the WWW do what I want it to do.	1.642	.000
I am in complete control when I use the WWW.	1.734	.000
If I had a problem using the WWW, I could solve it one way or another.	1.596	.042
I would prefer to learn new Web browser software packages on my own.	1.644	.030

Novice users wanted an experienced user nearby to answer questions, someone to show them how to use the Web, and to learn new browser packages. They did not feel in control or confident using the interface without assistance, despite their years of experience using computers and E-mail. They did not feel confident using the WWW despite their perceived satisfaction with the browser during the usability scenarios. Novice users made a distinction between the WWW and the browser experience, an indication that their uncertainty is focused on the mechanics of connecting to the WWW and of self-teaching to use Web software. The low affective scores among novice users confirmed that interfaces must be better designed for inexperienced users and instruction on how to use the WWW must be provided before using the Internet to deliver curriculum in classrooms.

Novice Web Users may also be Disadvantaged Learners

There are many ways to approach the issue of usability, the most common of which is to focus on information accessibility in the context of online documentation. Nabkel & Shafir used the phrase "metaphor and interaction dissonance" to describe the challenge of viewing dynamic, interactive movable objects (documents) with a static browser application. Developers of online curriculum can build on the strategies typically used for reading static, linear texts by providing Web users with spatial cues. These strategies include skimming, look backs, and rereading text to create a cognitive schematic of the information, with chapter headings and graphics as landmarks. The usability of an online document is directly related to these cohesion cues and ultimately to reading comprehension.

In online curriculum design, tasks, not the tools, are central. Designers should not focus on the interface, but on the ease with which users can access informational concepts. Yet information cannot be separated from the interface. If a user has trouble accessing the information or performing a task, then both the interface and the document structure are to blame, and both will have a negative effect on the user's attitude.

Summary

Many students are first introduced to the WWW in the classroom. Researchers have agreed about the benefits of incorporating Web technology in the classroom to expand resources and to allow worldwide communication. Technology, however must be incorporated with novice users in mind. To prevent low comprehension and further division of hardware have and have not faculty must consider the implication of merely transferring paper-based materials to the WWW. Following is a list of implications for novice Web users in any classroom environment:

1. Novice Web users need to be provided instruction on how to use a browser and how to install helper applications and plug ins.
2. Novice Web users need to be shown how the client - server architecture operates and how to recognize and resolve connection problems and error messages.
3. Faculty need to poll classes for novice and expert Web users, and pair novices and experts for the first few classroom projects in order that inexperienced users can gain confidence with Web technology.
4. Faculty need to clarify different connection tradeoffs from home and school and various browser features with text-only capabilities for faster downloading options.
5. Curriculum designers must include file sizes, particularly for large images and, audio and video clips, so that students can make informed decisions before downloading files.
6. Faculty are encouraged to poll classes for learning styles to be aware of positive and negative attitudes toward the WWW as a delivery vehicle.
7. Faculty need to poll classes for hardware and software access; they must be familiar with university computing center hours to ensure that all students have sufficient access to classroom materials presented only on the WWW.
8. Faculty need to integrate classroom goals and direct Web-based projects to ensure that students' time spent on the Internet is focused on browsing instead of on recreation.
9. Faculty need to redesign curriculum for Web delivery; they must also increasingly integrate images with captions and associate Web links to maximize the true potential of this technology.

10. Faculty should anticipate anxiety among novice Web users in classes using Web technology.
11. Faculty should anticipate over confidence among novice Web users in classes using Web technology.
12. Curriculum designers need to accommodate different browser limitations and configuration problems for students to ensure that all students can access the instruction.
13. Curriculum designers need to provide navigation in addition to browser navigation to facilitate associative learning across sections and within sections of instruction.

Novice and experienced Web users have provided critical data about the usability problems of interfaces. Most neophytes on the WWW took about 5 hours to learn from friends or in a course how to use a browser and author an Hypertext Markup Language (HTML). By observing and surveying this novice population, collected data help identify how to shorten the 5-hour learning curve and how to best meet instructional objectives on the WWW.

To successfully incorporate the WWW in education, designers and educational institutions must take human factors research into account. Because overly complex browser interface features detract from comprehension, browser designers must simplify the layout, graphic file format and size, and document structure when developing curriculum for novice Web users. Faculty must provide an introduction to the WWW before delivering information using this technology.

Netscape (version 1.1) was difficult for novice users to navigate: Subjects could not complete the five browser scenarios successfully. Users' familiarity with Web interface and ease of navigation using the browser increased usability performance and attitude. As demonstrated by observed behaviors and poor performance on usability trials, novice users' difficulty in accessing curriculum impeded comprehension. Thus, the browser, by impeding users' access to the curriculum, negatively affected comprehension of the material as well. Because the newest version of Netscape (now 4.0) is even more complex than the version (1.1) tested during these trials, more research on the usability of the browser by novice users is needed. As the Web user population continues to increase for all age groups, interface usability testing must continue and browser redesign take place to accommodate broader, more diverse audiences. Once browser interfaces are designed for non technical and younger populations, the WWW will become an even better learning resource.

10

INTERNET PORNOGRAPHY

Spectacular growth in availability of sexually explicit material on the Internet has created an unprecedented opportunity for individuals to have anonymous, cost-free, and unfettered access to an essentially unlimited range of sexually explicit texts, still and moving images, and audio materials. In a fashion never before imagined, men and women—and boys and girls can acquire sexually explicit content on the Internet, effortlessly and privately, as a direct expression of their sexual and personal characteristics and inclinations. Sexually explicit materials so obtained, in turn, may act to alter, not at all or more or less profoundly, the sexual and personal dispositions that incline individuals to seek out Internet sexuality in the first place.

Growth in access to Internet sexually explicit material challenges sexual science to conceptualize antecedents and consequences of experience with such content. One view based upon relevant theory and research suggests that antisocial personality characteristics will encourage some individuals to seek out antisocial sexually explicit materials from among those available on the Internet. The "goodness of fit" of antisocial personality characteristics with antisocial sexual content will, it is speculated, promote a tremendous depth of involvement in antisocial sexual stimuli. Individuals may lose awareness of the constraints of reality regarding enactment of antisocial sexual behavior, and uniquely strong negative effects of antisocial sexual content on the Internet may be seen among those predisposed to access such material.

A related view, also based upon relevant theory and research suggests that normal range individuals will ordinarily choose sexually explicit Internet materials which are not antisocial in nature. The "poorness of fit" of normal range personality characteristics with antisocial sexual content will, in fact, provoke avoidance of antisocial sexual stimuli, termination of contact with such stimuli if encountered, and rejection of the antisocial sexual messages of such stimuli. According to this analysis, most individuals have a lifetime learning history and set of expectancies about acceptable and unacceptable sexual behavior that is sufficient to deter them from accessing or acting on antisocial sexual content on the Internet.

The current discussion attempts to provide a conceptual and empirical context for considering antecedents and consequences of experience with Internet sexually explicit materials. At present, research concerning experience with Internet sexuality is at an early stage of development, and focused discussion of these issues may prove particularly valuable as sexual science moves toward more intensive study of this area. We begin this paper with a summary of some of what has been learned from existing research concerning sexually explicit materials, in contexts other than the Internet, and consider lessons from this work that may inform the study of Internet sexuality. A social psychological theory, the Sexual Behavior Sequence, is then applied as an heuristic guide in an initial effort to conceptualize a number of antecedents and consequences of experience with Internet sexuality. Our discussion closes with consideration of an agenda for future research concerning Internet sexually explicit materials. What follows, then, is a social psychological perspective—and certainly not the social psychological perspective—on aspects of Internet sexuality.

What do We Know About Defining Sexually Explicit Materials?

Conceptual and operational definition of terms is prerequisite to meaningful scientific discussion and research concerning sexually explicit materials, on or off the Internet. A three-part conceptualization of erotica, degrading pornography, and violent pornography has been suggested to guide theory and research in this area.

Definitions of erotica, degrading pornography, and violent pornography are based on the manifest content of sexually explicit materials. It is assumed that the content of sexually explicit material will be a distinguishing characteristic of such material and critical determinant of antecedents and consequences of experience with it. Content-based definitions of erotica generally hold that such material involves sexually explicit, non-degrading, and nonviolent portrayal of consensual sexual activity. Content-based definitions of degrading pornography hold that such material is sexually explicit and degrades, debases, and dehumanizes people, generally women, in a fashion that endorses such degradation. Content-based definitions of violent pornography assert that such material is sexually explicit and depicts and endorses the utility and normativeness of sexual violence, usually directed by men against women.

Definitions of erotica, degrading pornography, and violent pornography can be problematic. A primary concern is that achieving agreement about whether sexually explicit materials—on or off the Internet—fall into the broad categories of erotica, degrading pornography, or violent pornography, remains an unrealized objective. Although researchers such as Barron and Kimmell and Cowan and Dunn have studied the reliability of judgments of degradation and violence in small fragments of sexually explicit materials (e.g., 5-minute clips from full-length videos, and individual scenes in magazines, videos, and stories), our ability to reliably categorize complex and intact sexually explicit offerings, in the units in which they are experienced and interpreted by users, remains to be established. Moreover, whether or not sexually explicit materials that are categorized as erotica or as degrading pornography or violent pornography are actually spontaneously perceived and interpreted as such by consumers of sexually explicit material remains an entirely unanswered empirical question. Is it the case that what the researcher designates as violent pornography is spontaneously perceived and interpreted by the average male as an endorsement of the utility and normativeness of violence against women? Is it the case that what the researcher designates as erotica is spontaneously perceived and interpreted by the average female as a non-degrading sexual portrayal?

What lessons can be taken from efforts to define sexually explicit materials and applied to inform research on Internet sexuality? We would suggest that concerns regarding reliability and validity of definitions of sexually explicit materials can and should be addressed empirically, in order to facilitate meaningful study of Internet sexuality. Research concerning categorization of sexually explicit materials, in the complex and intact forms in which they are experienced, can address reliability concerns in an ecologically valid fashion.

Research concerning the crucial question of whether or not categorizations of erotica, degrading pornography, and violent pornography reflect spontaneous perceptions and interpretations of consumers of such material can address critical validity issues that have been raised. Until reliability and validity concerns about the definition of sexually explicit materials have been addressed, it will be difficult to map the content of Internet sexuality, to conceptualize or study effects of Internet sexually explicit materials, or to craft educational interventions or sociological policies concerning Internet sexuality.

What do We Know About the Prevalence of Sexually Explicit Materials?

Research interest in sexually explicit materials is historically associated with concern that such materials are enormously prevalent and are saturating society at an accelerating rate with each passing year. During the 1980s, a time of intense research interest in sexually explicit materials, a report in the Psychology of Women Quarterly informed readers that X-rated materials in the U.S. represented "an estimated $8 billion industry of misogyny per year" and the U.S. Attorney General's Commission reported that violent pornography was " the most prevalent form" of sexually explicit material. At the same time, a best-selling human sexuality textbook speculated that $1 billion per year of the U.S. sexually explicit media industry involved sales of child pornography and the important anti-pornography documentary film, Not a Love Story, informed its viewers that the sexually explicit media are controlled by organized crime.

Systematic studies of the prevalence of sexually explicit materials appear at first glance to verify views about the saturation of western society with violent pornography. A closer look at research findings in this area, however, provides a cautionary tale of conflicting and inconsistent results. We find, for example, that Malamuth and Spinner report a steady increase in sexual violence in Playboy and Penthouse across the 1970s, from about 1% to 5% of all text and pictures. Scott and Cuvelier , however, studied some of the same magazines over some of the same years and found that, over all of the 30 years of Playboy's publication, sexually violent pictures (.16 per issue) or cartoons (.58 per issue) were extraordinarily rare, and were actually decreasing in frequency of occurrence over time.

In the realm of sexually explicit videos, Cowan reported that fully 51% of X-rated videos sampled portrayed the rape of a woman, whereas Palys ,Garcia and Milano found vastly less sexual violence in such videos, and Palys determined that levels of sexual violence in X-rated videos had been declining across the decade under study. Other researchers report very high levels of sexual violence overall in sexually explicit magazines, videos, and Internet sex story postings, but at the same time note that the perpetrators of sexual violence in these media are usually or often women (65%, 49%, and 42% of perpetrators of sexual violence were women in magazines, videos, and Internet postings, respectively).

Initial reports of the prevalence of sexually explicit material on the Internet are eerily reminiscent of initial reports of the prevalence of print and video pornography. For example, Rimm's (1995) Georgetown Law Review paper, "A Survey of 917,410 Images, Descriptions, Short Stories, and Animations Downloaded 8.5 Million Times by Consumers in Over 2000 Cities " The Time magazine cover story was quickly followed by passage of the U.S. Communications Decency Act of 1996, designed to suppress the flood of Internet pornography, but the Communications Decency Act itself was quickly declared unconstitutional. Current reports indicate variously that the online pornography industry will gross

$366 million by 2001 or that it already grosses in excess of $1 billion ("Blue Money," 1999), and reports indicate that a spectacular 69% of all e-commerce involves the purchase of sexual materials ("Blue Money," 1999). Other sources report that 15% of all Internet users accessed one of the top five "Adult" websites in a recent month, that sex is the most frequently searched topic on the Internet, and that all of the top eight word searches on the Internet involve pornography . In another example, Canada's national newspaper of record recently printed a two-part series entitled "The Triple-X Crisis. Is Pornography Out of Control?". This report informs readers that 3.8 million Canadians visited an Internet sex site in October of 2000 and reports that the average user visits Internet sex sites on 4 days per month. We note in passing that taking these statistics seriously requires us to believe that approximately 25% of all Canadian males, aged birth to death, visited an Internet sexuality site last month, and did so on an average of 4 different days.

In addition to inconsistencies and prima questionable claims in research on the prevalence of sexually explicit materials, on and off the Internet, we note the nearly complete absence of research on the central and obvious issue of consumer preference for different types of sexual content. In an effort to address the critical question of what sort of sexually explicit material, if any, men might choose to see in a free-choice situation, Bogaert conducted a very simple and very informative study. Undergraduate males who were already participating in a study were given the opportunity to sign up, for experimental credit, for additional research that would involve viewing their choice of 14 videos. Subjects were permitted to choose to see videos depicting common sexual acts, novel sexual acts, sexually insatiable females, sexual violence, or child pornography. Results showed that undergraduate men's modal choice—51% of all men—was to decline to see any sexually explicit video, either because they did not need further experimental credit or because they were simply not interested. The second most frequent choice (15% of all men) was to see erotic depictions that were nonviolent and involved female sexual insatiability. The next most frequent choices were to view a control film, Saturday Night Live (8%), a video that portrayed sexual novelty including sexual activity with animals (8%), or a video depicting common sexual acts (7%). Men's least common choices, in this free-choice setting, were to see sexually violent videos (4%) or child pornography (3%). Bogaert's research emphasizes the central but generally ignored point that contact with sexually explicit material is a self-regulated choice which may be exercised or declined by individuals and that experience with sexually explicit materials should be studied in such a context by sexual scientists. When ecologically valid opportunities to choose are given, as is the case in this single study, the modal choice was not to bother to see any sexually explicit material at all, and the least common choice was to view violent pornography or child sexual activity. Such findings place an important qualification on experimental research concerning the effects of sexually explicit stimuli, in which exposure to such stimuli is enforced on individuals.

What lessons can be taken from attempts to assess the prevalence of sexually explicit materials and applied to inform research on Internet sexuality? First, the record strongly suggests that it is important to avoid moral panic and premature pronouncements about the saturation of society with Internet pornography. Wildly conflicting statements, often doubtful on their face, about the extraordinary amount of sexually explicit material that is available, the extraordinary amount of such material that is sold, and the extraordinary proportion of all e-commerce accounted for by sales of sexual material, are quickly accepted. Such claims can just as quickly turn into a source of scientific embarrassment when the data are closely examined. Second, it is instructive to note that a degree of precision is warranted in assessments of the prevalence of sexually explicit materials on the Internet. Categories of erotica, degrading pornography, and violent pornography are almost always collapsed into the single category of "pornography" reflecting a presumably homogeneous " industry of misogyny". Such collapsing of all sexually explicit materials into a single category of "pornography" eliminates our ability to map out the prevalence of different types of sexually explicit materials on the Internet, or to consider effects of different types of sexually explicit content on the Internet, in any meaningful fashion, even ignoring serious reliability and validity concerns articulated earlier. Finally, Bogaert's research reminds us that use of erotic or pornographic materials is an individual choice. Studies of prevalence of different types of sexually explicit material on the Internet must include studies of consumer preference for various types of sexually explicit content in free-choice settings.

What do We Know About Antecedents and Consequences of Experience with Sexually Explicit Materials?

In working toward an understanding of Internet sexually explicit materials, it would be useful to consider research concerning personality characteristics that incline individuals to seek out sexually explicit media. It would also be useful to consider research findings concerning effects of contact with sexually explicit media on individuals who have chosen to consume such material.

With respect to antecedents of self-directed experience with sexually explicit media, perhaps the most comprehensive study of personality factors that incline individuals to seek out such materials was conducted by Bogaert. Bogaert assessed a range of relevant individual differences in a sample of undergraduate men, including aggression, altruism, delinquency, dominance, hypermasculinity, Machiavellianism, psychoticism, sensation seeking, erotophobia-erotophilia, and attraction to sexual aggression. Men's sexual experience, past sexual media exposure, history of sexual aggression, and current sexual behavior were assessed as well. The men were then asked to choose which of a number of videos they would like to view. The videos were presented to participants with titles and descriptions which established them as involving common sexual acts, novel sexual acts, sexually insatiable females, sexual violence, and children engaging in sexual acts, or as nonviolent, non-sexual, or violent non-sexual video material. After statistically controlling for social desirability, none of the individual difference characteristics assessed were associated with men's tendencies to choose to see the sexually violent or common sexual acts videos. Choice of female sexual insatiability videos was associated with erotophilia; choice of child sexual videos, which was very rare (3% of all males chose to see this stimulus), was associated with history of exposure to sexual media and with the personality traits of aggression and dominance; and choice of novel sexual acts videos was associated with history of exposure to sexually explicit media. Attraction to sexual aggression was not correlated with choices to view any of the categories of sexual media under study.

A single study known to us is relevant to the question of the antecedents of self-regulated exposure to Internet sexuality. Barak examined individual difference correlates of choosing to access sexually explicit Internet sites in a sample of university men. These investigators found no association of men's social desirability, sensation seeking, attitudes toward women, rape myth acceptance, hypermasculinity, or erotophobia-erotophilia with time spent surfing sexually explicit Internet sites. The only correlate of the time men spent surfing sexually explicit Internet sites was men's past experience with sexually explicit media.

Other research of some relevance to the question of the antecedents of consumption of sexually explicit materials tells us that convicted sex criminals are either less likely or at least not differentially likely to have experience with sexually explicit media and that it is egalitarian and not sexist attitudes toward women which are correlated with viewing sexually explicit movies or videos in natural settings. Still other research indicates that in general, erotophilic individuals, who show dispositionally positive affective, evaluative, and approach responses to sexuality, are more likely than erotophobic individuals to choose to consume sexually explicit materials, and that male (vs. female) gender is associated with more frequent consumption of sexually explicit material.

With respect to research concerning the effects of exposure to sexually explicit media on individuals who have chosen to have contact with such material, research is limited. We do know that in two separate studies reported by Barak amount of self-directed exposure to Internet sexually explicit sites had no significant effects on post-exposure measures of university men's rape myth acceptance, attitudes toward women, acceptance of women as managers, or on a measure of likelihood of sexual harassment. In another potentially relevant study, Malamuth examined factors such as family violence, delinquency, attitudes supporting violence, sexual promiscuity, hostile masculinity, and pornography use—defined as amount of exposure to sexually explicit magazines—as correlates of sexual aggression against women, in a national sample of men enrolled in post secondary education. The authors report that men who were highest in hostile masculinity, sexual promiscuity, and pornography use as defined in this research were most likely to report a history of sexual aggression against women. At the same time, however, the researchers note that"... we cannot conclude on the basis of these analyses that pornography use is a cause or an outcome of sexual aggressive tendencies". Characteristics of this research, including its cross-sectional design and coding of sexually explicit magazine use as "pornography," seriously limit the ability of this study to address the question of effects of self-directed exposure to different types of sexually explicit materials, on or off the Internet. Findings that individuals who seek out sexually explicit movies or videos in natural settings have egalitarian and not sexist attitudes toward women, and findings for a lack of association of sexual criminality with exposure to sexually explicit media are also not consistent with a view that self-directed exposure to sexually explicit materials results in anti-woman attitudinal shifts or antisocial sexual behavior.

As an additional and crude estimate of consequences of exposure to sexually explicit Internet materials on individuals who seek contact with such content, in Figure 1 we plot rates of reported forcible rape in the United States from 1995 to 1999. This time interval is by all accounts a period of exponential growth in the availability and use of all forms of Internet sexually explicit materials. Although open to a variety of interpretations, we note that the rate of reported forcible rape in the U.S. fell consistently and significantly throughout this time period of spectacular increase in access to and use of Internet sexually explicit materials of all kinds.

Although there is an enormous amount of research concerning the effects of experimentally enforced exposure to sexually explicit materials on individuals who have not chosen to see such materials, extrapolating findings from such research is a risky proposition. Effects of Internet or other sexually explicit materials are almost certainly a joint function of the personality characteristics of the individual who seeks out such materials and of exposure to such materials. Experiments involving enforced exposure to sexually explicit materials ignore the influence of synergistic or buffering personality characteristics that might amplify or attenuate effects of exposure and which are correlated with the inclination to seek or to avoid sexually explicit material. Findings from enforced exposure experimental paradigms, therefore, cannot be generalized readily to assumptions about effects of self-directed, real world exposure to Internet sexually explicit materials.

What lessons can we carry forward from research concerning antecedents and consequences of exposure to sexually explicit materials to inform research concerning Internet sexuality?

First, we note that research on antecedents of self-directed exposure to sexually explicit materials is very limited, and that use of an ecologically valid research paradigm that examines individual difference correlates of choice of Internet sexually explicit materials is needed. Existing research has already identified a variety of individual difference correlates of choice of sexually explicit media, on and off the Internet, that are potentially highly relevant to moderating effects of exposure to such materials.

Second, we note that research concerning effects of exposure to sexually explicit materials on those who choose to consume them is also rare, and existing findings by and large fail to confirm fears of strong antisocial effects of self-directed exposure to sexually explicit media. A significant lesson to carry forward for emerging research on Internet sexuality involves the importance of conducting ecologically valid research concerning effects of self-regulated exposure to Internet sexually explicit materials on individuals who choose to consume them. Such research will be able to capture compound effects of the personality characteristics of those inclined to access Internet sexuality and of Internet sexually explicit materials per se.

Social Psychological Perspective on Internet

As sexual scientists confront the challenge of understanding antecedents and consequences of contact with Internet sexually explicit materials, we believe there is considerable advantage to be gained by applying social psychological theory to guide conceptual and research efforts. A number of relevant theories (e.g., Sexual Behavior Sequence, Byrne, 1977; Theory of Reasoned Action, Fishbein & Ajzen, 1975; Excitation Transfer Theory, Zillmann & Bryant, 1984;

Social-Cognitive Theory, Bandura, 1986; Confluence Model, Malamuth et al., 2001) could serve as a basis for understanding factors which would incline an individual to access Internet sexually explicit materials, and could be extended as a basis for conjecture about how access to Internet sexually explicit materials will condition the individual's future sexual behavior. We have chosen the Sexual Behavior Sequence as a basis for conceptualizing antecedents and consequences of experience with Internet sexually explicit materials for a number of reasons. The Sexual Behavior Sequence focuses on understanding sexual stimuli; the arousal, affective, cognitive, and behavioral responses they evoke; and the effect of these responses in conditioning the future approach or avoidance of sexual stimuli and sexual behavior. As such, the Sexual Behavior Sequence provides a conceptually comprehensive heuristic guide for an initial attempt to understand some of the factors that will incline an individual to access Internet sexually explicit material and for understanding some of the internal psychological and external behavioral responses to such stimuli. In addition, the Sexual Behavior Sequence directly addresses the question of how the effects of experience with Internet sexuality may influence an individual's future sexual behavior. Although we believe that the Sexual Behavior Sequence is a conceptually comprehensive heuristic guide that addresses both antecedents and consequences of experience with Internet sexuality, we emphasize that it is utilized here only as a conceptual roadmap of constructs which are potentially important in the study of Internet sexuality and as a basis for hypothesis generation.

The Sexual Behavior Sequence

The Sexual Behavior Sequence is a social psychological model of the antecedents and consequences of sexual behavior that can be applied to conceptualizing experience with Internet sexuality. The Sexual Behavior Sequence asserts that individuals respond to unconditioned and conditioned erotic cues with sexual arousal and affective and cognitive responses. Sexual arousal, affect, and cognition may motivate and guide preparatory sexual behaviors that affect the likelihood of overt sexual behaviors. Overt sexual behaviors, according to the model, have subjectively positive or negative consequences that will influence the future probability of the responses that led to the sexual behavior in the first place, by way of a feedback loop specified by the model.

Sexual Stimuli—Sexual Arousal—Sexual Behavior

According to the Sexual Behavior Sequence, individuals respond to unconditioned sexual stimuli with physiological sexual arousal. Unconditioned erotic stimuli can include tactile stimulation of the genitals, exposure to pheromones, and possibly, visual sexual cues such as exposure to the genitals or breasts or observation of copulatory behavior. The Sexual Behavior Sequence also asserts that any other discriminable stimulus which is associated with an unconditioned erotic stimulus can become a conditioned erotic stimulus with the capacity to elicit physiological sexual arousal itself.

According to the Sexual Behavior Sequence, individuals who come into contact with erotic stimuli and who are sufficiently sexually aroused for a sufficient period of time are motivated to engage in preparatory sexual behavior that will increase the likelihood of overt sexual behavior. Preparatory sexual behaviors which increase the likelihood of overt sexual behavior can involve actions such as locking one's bedroom door and plugging in a vibrator, making sexual overtures to an opposite-sex or same-sex partner, or seeking sexual companionship in a singles bar or in an Internet chat room. If preparatory sexual behaviors are successful, sexual behavior will result, and sexual behaviors have outcomes that may be experienced as subjectively positive or negative events. Outcomes are assumed to feed back into the system to condition the future greater or lesser likelihood of the chain of events that led to the sexual behavior and outcome in question.

Considering only the erotic stimulus – physiological arousal – preparatory behavior – sexual behavior – outcome level of the Sexual Behavior Sequence, let us turn to the example of a neophyte male Internet user. Having discovered JJJ's Thumbnail Post in the course of idle surfing, our Internet user has viewed text, images, and video clips depicting a variety of stimulus themes – including consensual heterosexual intercourse, bondage and discipline, interracial anal intercourse, urination, and cumshots, all depicted as discriminable stimulus accompaniments of unconditioned erotic stimuli such as copulatory behavior and breast and genital imagery. Our Internet explorer settles on a stimulus theme that he finds idiosyncratically to be arousing—cumshot still and moving images of a male ejaculating onto the face, hair, breasts, and vulva of a female. Over time, the Internet user finds that cumshot themes in general have become a conditioned erotic stimulus with the capacity to elicit high levels of physiological sexual arousal and with the ability to motivate preparatory sexual behaviors, sexual behaviors, and outcomes. Whether or not the acquisition of the cumshot theme as a conditioned erotic stimulus will ever be translated into covert fantasy or overt behavior involving ejaculation onto a woman's face or body will be a function of affective and cognitive responses which are simultaneously evoked by the sexually explicit Internet stimulus category in question and whose roles are also specified by the Sexual Behavior Sequence.

Sexual Stimuli—Affective Responses—Sexual Behavior

The Sexual Behavior Sequence asserts that individuals respond to erotic stimuli with affective and evaluative responses as well as with physiological sexual arousal. According to the Sexual Behavior Sequence, affective and evaluative responses to sexual stimuli, along with physiological sexual arousal responses to such stimuli, will together influence the occurrence of preparatory sexual behavior, overt sexual behavior, and the subjective outcome of such behavior.

From the perspective of the Sexual Behavior Sequence, individuals acquire affective and evaluative responses to erotic stimuli as a function of the association of erotic stimuli with rewarding or punishing experiences over the life span. An individual who has experienced predominantly rewarding experiences in association with sexuality is expected to develop a generalized trait disposition of erotophilia and should respond to sexual cues with positive affect and evaluations. An individual who has experienced predominantly punishing experiences in association with sexuality is expected to develop a generalized trait disposition of erotophobia and should respond to sexual cues with negative affect and evaluations. Positive affective and evaluative responses to sexual stimuli should incline the individual to engage in preparatory sexual behavior and sexual behavior and to experience the outcome of this sexual behavior as subjectively positive. Such a positive outcome will strengthen the future likelihood of further contact with similar sexual stimuli, the future likelihood of similar arousal and affective and evaluative responses, similar preparatory and overt sexual behaviors, and similar outcomes. In contrast, negative affective and evaluative responses to sexual stimuli should motivate the sexually stimulated individual to avoid the sort of preparatory sexual behavior and overt sexual behavior suggested by the sexual stimulus and to experience the sexual stimulus, and any arousal or behavior which it eventuates, as hedonically negative events that will condition future avoidance of sexual stimulation of the sort that triggered this sequence of responses.

According to the Sexual Behavior Sequence, then, experience with Internet sexually explicit materials will be a self-regulated activity that will take place in part as a function of an individual's erotophobic or erotophilic disposition to respond to Internet sexuality with positive or negative affect and evaluations. Erotophilic individuals should seek out and enjoy Internet sexually explicit materials, and may incorporate what is acquired from Internet sexually explicit materials into their preparatory and overt sexual behaviors, and should enjoy these behaviors, all else being equal. This sequence of responses, involving additional pairings of sexuality with positive affective responses, should also strengthen the erotophilic disposition which provoked it in the first place. Erotophobic individuals, in contrast, will experience contact with Internet sexually explicit materials as an emotionally negative event and will evaluate such materials negatively and avoid contact with them. By extension, erotophobic individuals will also avoid preparatory and overt sexual behaviors related to Internet sexually explicit materials. This sequence of responses, involving additional pairing of sexuality with negative affect, should strengthen the individual's erotophobic disposition and his or her inclination to avoid Internet sexually explicit materials in the future.

Let us return to our example of the Internet user who has acquired a sexual arousal response to the theme of ejaculation on a woman's face or body. Let us further assume, in accord with the Sexual Behavior Sequence, that the individual in question is erotophilic and that in fact it is his affective and evaluative positively to sexuality which brought him to surf Internet sex sites and to acquire conditioned sexual arousal to cumshots in the first place. Sexual arousal and positive affective and evaluative responses to cumshot stimuli should, according to our model and all else being equal, affect the individual's preparatory sexual behavior, sexual behavior, outcomes, and future probability of the sequence of events that provoked them. In the current case, the erotophilic individual likely has an erotophilic partner, and the individual may be motivated to engage in a preparatory sexual behavior which involves discussion with a partner of incorporating an arousing new sexual activity—say, ejaculation onto her breasts—during sexual intercourse. Such discussion could be instrumental in the occurrence of a sexual behavior of this sort and could provoke a positive personal and dyadic outcome that would strengthen the future likelihood of this entire sequence of events. Alternatively, and almost certainly more realistically, the individual who is sexually aroused and effectively positive to the prospect of ejaculation on a partner's body might receive such a negative interpersonal reaction to either the discussion or performance of this behavior that the outcome would be profoundly negative and result in the future unlikelihood of anything remotely associated with cumshot activity. Or, the individual in question who is sexually stimulated by the cumshot theme might chose a preparatory behavior such as a generic sexual overture to a partner which results in a conventional sexual behavior such as sexual intercourse, accompanied by a covert sexual fantasy of cumshot activity. This personally rewarding outcome would condition the increased likelihood of this sequence of events in the future without involving potentially negative partner responses. For the individual who is aroused by the prospect of ejaculation onto a partner's body and who is effectively and evaluatively positive concerning this activity, the question of whether the overt or covert version or any version of this scenario will be enacted will depend heavily on the individual's cognitive responses to this category of sexual behavior, as specified by the Sexual Behavior Sequence and discussed following.

Sexual Stimuli—Cognitive Responses—Sexual Behavior

According to the Sexual Behavior Sequence, erotic stimuli evoke categories of cognitive responses that—together with arousal and affective responses—determine preparatory sexual behavior, overt sexual behavior, and the outcomes of such behavior. Cognitive responses to erotic stimuli include informational responses, expectative responses, and imaginative responses. Informational responses to sexual stimuli consist of beliefs about sexual activity, and expectative responses are subjective probability estimates concerning the outcomes of sexual activity. Imaginative responses to sexual stimulation involve script-like representations of entire sexual episodes which may be used to test out safely and in private contemplation a pattern of behavior that one is considering implementing, or which may be used to experience, solely in private contemplation, a behavior that one would never consider actually implementing.

From the perspective of the Sexual Behavior Sequence, information, expectancies, and imaginative responses will heavily affect an individual's experience with Internet sexually explicit materials. Consider our example of the erotophilic Internet suffer who has acquired sexual arousal responses to the stimulus category of ejaculation onto a female's face or body. From the perspective of the Sexual Behavior Sequence, the individual's informational, expectative, and imaginative responses to the prospect of ejaculation on a partner's face or body will determine the nature of his preparatory sexual behavior, sexual behavior, and outcomes. Assume, for example, that our protagonist is sexually aroused and affectively positive about the possibility of engaging in sexual activities that include ejaculation onto his partner. Assume as well that (a) the surfer in question believes that ejaculation onto his partner's breasts is a relatively reserved form of this behavior, as suggested by depictions he has seen on the Internet (an informational response); (b) the surfer in question believes that his partner would probably respond tolerantly to discussion of this activity and to it's actual occurrence, as suggested by past experience with the partner (an expectative response); and (c) the surfer in question can imagine a sequence of cumshot activity behaviors producing a positive outcome for himself and his partner (an imaginative response). In such a case, contact with Internet sexually explicit stimuli may trigger overt experimentation with behavior and possibly a positive outcome and increased future likelihood of such behavior. If, in contrast, the individual's informational, expectative, and imaginative responses suggest that ejaculation onto the partner's breasts would almost certainly provoke negative responses which are vividly imagined, the individual might chose to confine his cumshot activity to covert fantasy accompaniment of conventional sexual activity as discussed earlier. Or, the surfer in question might choose to redirect his sexual fantasy to what he imagines to be a more acceptable behavior. In either case, it is the avoidance of an overt sexual behavior that would have a positive outcome and that would continue in the future.

All Together Now: Arousal, Affective, Cognitive, and Behavioral Responses to Internet Sexually Explicit Materials

From the perspective of the Sexual Behavior Sequence, exposure to Internet sexually explicit materials may trigger the acquisition of conditioned sexual arousal responses, affective and evaluative responses, informational and expectative responses, and sexual fantasy responses. These internal psychological reactions to Internet sexually explicit stimuli will together determine the occurrence and nature of preparatory sexual behavior, overt sexual behavior, the outcome of such behavior, and the future probability of sexual behavior, including future contact with Internet sexually explicit materials. The Sexual Behavior Sequence thus conceptualizes experience with Internet sexually explicit material as a choice made by an active perceiver and interpreter of such material. The Sexual Behavior Sequence also emphasizes that the individual brings a lifetime learning history, involving emotional responses to sexuality, beliefs about sexual activity, and expectations and imagination concerning the outcomes of sexual behaviors, to experience with Internet sexuality. In contrast to implicit "Monkey see, monkey do" assumptions which seem to have guided much research on exposure to erotica and pornography, the Sexual Behavior Sequence conceptualizes contact with Internet sexually explicit material as a self-regulated event which will occur or not occur as a function of an individual's arousal, affective, and cognitive responses to sexuality. The individual's internal affective and cognitive responses to Internet sexually explicit materials will determine whether or not future contact with Internet sexuality is sought or avoided, and will determine the sort of behavioral responses which are or are not provoked by experience with Internet sexually explicit materials. Finally, experience with Internet sexuality should also affect the future development an individual's arousal, affective and cognitive responses to sexuality and his or her future sexual behavior, most likely in a direction which is consistent with the individual's preexisting response tendencies in these areas. Understanding an individual's experience with Internet sexually explicit material requires consideration of multiple and simultaneous arousal, affective, and cognitive responses of the individual to sexual stimulation.

The Sexual Behavior Sequence can also be applied as a conceptual guide for clinical interventions designed to assist individuals who have self-designated or socially-designated problems with Internet sexuality, including excessive and interfering preoccupation with Internet sexually explicit materials, inappropriate behavior stemming from contact with Internet sexuality, or personally or socially problematic replacement of sexual activity on the Internet for sexual activity with a partner. In such cases, diagnostic focus on arousal, affective, and cognitive factors that provoke or permit dysfunctional behavior might prove useful in understanding the problem and in formulating an intervention plan. Is the individual who is preoccupied with Internet sexually explicit materials in a way that is interfering with his or her work and relationships and finances involved in such maladaptive activity because Internet sexuality is more arousing to the individual than competing, non-interfering sources of sexual arousal? Is the individual more affectively positive to Internet sexuality than he or she is affectively negative to the consequences of excessive involvement? Is the individual unable to anticipate and imagine the individual consequences and social stigma occasioned by his or her behavior? And would interventions targeted at augmenting access to adaptive sources of sexual arousal, at increasing affective negativity to the consequences of his or her activity, and at encouraging the individual to imagine the negative reactions of employers and partners, be effective in assisting the individual to avoid excessive and interfering use of Internet sexually explicit materials?

Sources of Internet Sexually Explicit Materials

In crafting an agenda for future research on Internet sexually explicit materials which integrates the issues discussed in this paper, we prioritize conceptually driven and ecologically valid research, guided by the Sexual Behavior Sequence and other relevant models. This agenda will focus on examining effects of preexisting arousal, affective, and cognitive responses to sexuality on self-regulated consumption of Internet sexually explicit materials in free-choice settings that model well the natural environment. This research agenda will also examine effects of self-regulated experience with Internet sexually explicit materials on individuals' arousal, affective, and cognitive responses to sexuality, and examine how effects on these internal responses may contribute to changes in individuals' covert sexual fantasy and overt sexual behavior over extended periods of time.

Based upon the Sexual Behavior Sequence and related research, we hypothesize that individuals with strong preexisting sexual arousal responses to sexually explicit materials, and strong preexisting positive affective and cognitive responses to sexuality, will engage in relatively greater self-regulated consumption of Internet sexually explicit materials. Based upon the current analysis, we also anticipate that experience with Internet sexuality will reinforce individuals' preexisting arousal, affective, and cognitive responses to sexuality. Those who approach Internet sexuality with strong arousal responses and positive affective and cognitive responses to sexuality will find these response tendencies strengthened. Those who approach Internet sexuality with weak arousal responses and negative affective and cognitive responses to sexuality will find these response dispositions made more pronounced. Finally, based on the Sexual Behavior Sequence, we expect that experience with Internet sexuality will affect individuals' covert imaginative and overt sexual behavior in a fashion that is consistent with his or her arousal, affective, and cognitive responses to sexuality. Individuals who approach Internet sexuality with strong arousal responses and positive affective and cognitive responses to sexuality will be more inclined to incorporate elements of Internet sexual scenarios into their covert and overt sexual behavior, all else being equal, and in accord with the expected outcomes of these behavioral choices. In contrast, individuals who approach Internet sexuality with weak arousal responses and negative affective and cognitive responses to sexuality will be unlikely to incorporate Internet sexual scenarios into their covert or overt sexual behavior.

By happy coincidence, existing Internet technology provides an exceedingly suitable methodology for executing the research agenda we have articulated. Assume, for example, that a researcher is able to create a panel of Internet users, representing both sexes, and sampling the age range from 18 to 65. Further assume that, after appropriate informed consent, the panel of Internet users completes a series of assessments of baseline sexual arousal responses to a range of sexually explicit stimuli, and a set of measures of affective—evaluative, informational—expectative, and imaginative responses to sexuality. Assume as well that the research subjects complete a profile of current sexual behavior and attitudinal and behavioral measures—such as attitudes toward women, rape myth acceptance, sexually coercive behaviors, and inappropriate and interfering utilization of Internet sexuality—which represent potential negative outcomes of self-regulated exposure to Internet sexually explicit materials. This battery of baseline assessments would be completed online. Participants would then be given free access to the Internet for a period of, say, 1 or 2 years, with informed consent to the proviso that software installed on their computers will sample Internet utilization at given intervals of time and will automatically and anonymously communicate these data to the researchers. Moreover, halfway through the period of study and at its conclusion the researchers will conduct repeat Internet-based assessments of arousal responses to sexually explicit stimuli and affective—evaluative, informational—expectative, and imaginative responses to sexuality. In addition, subjects will again complete assessments of sexual behavior, attitudes toward women, likelihood of rape, coercive sexual behavior, and inappropriate and interfering utilization of Internet sexuality at these intervals.

A research strategy with these characteristics would permit empirical study of such central questions as the self-regulation of experience with Internet sexually explicit materials, in relation to preexisting individual difference characteristics, and the mapping over extended periods of time of self-regulated experience with Internet sexually explicit materials by men and women across the age range. Such a research strategy would also permit prospective examination of the effects of self-regulated exposure to Internet sexuality over time on arousal, affective, cognitive, and behavioral responses, and on a range of possible antisocial attitudinal and behavioral outcomes of self-regulated experience with Internet sexually explicit materials. It is our hope that this research agenda will contribute to conceptually and empirically fruitful investigation which will inform understanding, policy, and practice concerning Internet sexuality in coming years.

11

Cybersex

This paper itself describes and analyzes two kinds of on-line relationships, as a thought-experiment to explore conflicting intuitions about what matters in personal relationships. Thinking about "virtual" affairs conducted in the medium of cyberspace allows us to consider the importance of the disposition of bodies in personal relationships. By appeal to these case-studies, I will argue that although sexual and emotional infidelities may well be of concern within particular relationships, feminist attention should be focused currently on a different mode of fidelity, "practical fidelity," which emphasizes interactions between individuals conducted in physical space. Virtual relationships should not now be regarded as having the same significance as body-based relationships.

Before turning to the case studies, let me sketch the traditional Christian model of marriage, which provides the contrasting backdrop for the discussion below. This model presents a comprehensive account of what committed relationships are like and should be like. A committed relationship must be a heterosexual marriage properly constituted in the eyes of the state and the Lord, with the wife subordinated to her husband. The spouses should live together and provide a stable and pious home for their children, whose procreation and upbringing are the primary goals of the relationship. Marriage is an essential part of a flourishing human life. Once overlaid with the bourgeois ideology of romantic love in the mid-nineteenth century, marriage appears as a woman's destiny, and the necessary support to a man's achievement of his primary goal of success in the public sphere. Sex becomes an emotional as well as physical fusion of selves.

Clearly, many features of this model are unacceptable on feminist grounds, notably: it is inegalitarian (a wife is graciously to submit to her husband), heterosexist (only opposite sexes are to marry) and pronatalist (the only good sex is procreative sex and women's natural and best role is to bear and rear as many children as possible).

However, this traditional understanding of what a committed relationship is and should be continues to dominate North American culture. For example, to the extent that the popular media were able to sympathize with the companion of the late Gianni Versace, it was by configuring his situation, "as if he had lost his spouse." Alternative forms of committed relationships are made popularly intelligible by comparison with the marriage model. Moreover, many important social, legal, and economic benefits are only available to those whose relationships at least appear to conform to the marriage model.

At the same time, there are hints that the ideological power of this model is waning. For example, despite the protestations of the Right, in some parts of the U.S. there is some acceptance of gay and lesbian marriages. Some companies now grant benefits to "domestic partners," whether or not married and heterosexual. Currently, the U.S. military is debating whether to downgrade its judgment of the seriousness of adultery. As the Clinton sex scandal plays out, there has been public debate about what counts as sexual, and hence as adulterous, activity. The dominant story about the role of sex in a committed relationship as properly procreative and the correlative definition of sex are in question. Again, there is demographic evidence that the marriage model is no longer descriptively adequate for many relationships.

In this cultural context, there is a need for feminist theorists to provide an alternative framework for exploring the meaning of committed relationships. One set of questions revolves around the nature and significance of different forms of infidelity. As a thought experiment to explore intuitions about what commitment requires, let us consider the following two cases:

1. The on-line erotic affair One partner, B, in a conventional committed relationship (e.g., they have lived together for years, they have a joint bank account, etc.), catches the other, A, typing at a steamed-up computer screen. Over A's shoulder, B reads, "Ooh C baby, come back to the hot tub and let me nibble your lobes." A is too absorbed to notice B reading the cyberchum's, C's, lascivious response.
2. The on-line romantic affair (the affair of the cyber heart). Imagine the same set-up, but this time B reads as A types, "privy as you are, my dearest C, to my innermost secrets, you already know how much I have yearned all day, to resume our conversation of last night." A is too absorbed to notice B reading the cyberchum's, C's, mawkish reply.

Should we regard cybersexual affairs as a species of adultery, an impermissible form of sexual betrayal, and cyber-romances as a comparable species of emotional infidelity, call it "emotional adultery"? Is A an adulterer as accused, has B truly been betrayed as B believes, and is C, the cyberchum, really a relationship-wrecker? I will look at each of these issues, and show that there are good prima facie reasons for contemporary feminists to respond in very different ways.

The Case of Cyberlust

Assume that B is upset and accuses the cyber luster, A, of a sexual betrayal incompatible with their committed relationship. Talking about sex on-line just is sex. The accused offers the following defense: "Cybersex is not really sex in the relevant sense. This `affair' involves no physical contact, let alone intimate genital contact, with another person, any more than reading Play person does. I had no intention of planning to meet C in the flesh. Hence, I have not sexually betrayed our relationship."

B responds: "It is not fair to compare cybersex with reading Play person on your own. Your sexual arousal is premised on the belief that there is someone, C, who is responding in real time to your advances—that's why you sought an interactive chat room, rather than a solitary reading of pornography. You would not find it nearly as exciting if it turned out that C was just a bot, programmed to respond appropriately to verbal cues."

A may concede this point, but continue the defense thus: "Yes, the virtual involvement of another is important to my cyber project, but you are making a category mistake to accuse me of sexual infidelity. You are conflating collaborative writing about sex with sexual activity, fiction with fact. My correspondent is just co-author, intended audience and critic. Of course writing about sex feels sexy, and that's why I do it, but it isn't sex. What was happening on-line was a fictional description of sex between two fictional characters: my on-line persona A* and C's on-line persona, C*. Real sex happens between two real people in the flesh. Real adultery requires real sex."

A's defense now rests primarily on the claim that paradigmatic sexual activity involves physical contact, unmediated by technology. B may counter: "Why must paradigmatic sexual activity involve physical compresence of bodies? You might not be upset to find me on the phone to a stranger with a sex toy in my hand, but what if you found me clad in a virtual reality suit, gasping with pleasure at C's cyber touch? If the pleasure centers in my brain are activated as a result of C's stimulation, the length of the causal chain and the nature of the links does not matter. All of our sensory contact with others is ultimately a matter of moving electrons; it is arbitrary to delineate the forbidden sexual contact zone, as you do, in terms of the fleshly outline of the body."

Let us put this quarrel between A and B on hold, and review their positions. Let us assume both A and B are feminists. What reasons might each have for maintaining their respective views about what counts as sex?

A maintains that paradigmatic sex involves physical contact primarily for prudential reasons. A has just been reading Othello and reflecting on the threat male sexual jealousy poses to women's safety. Many studies suggest that male sexual possessiveness is a leading motive for male battery of present and ex- female partners. In this context, A worries that endorsing the view that sex need not involve physical contact will leave women with no way of defending themselves against male accusations of sexual infidelity: simply proving that Desdemona was nowhere near Cassio cannot disprove sexual activity. Further, if sexually provocative behavior need involve no bodily displacement at all, how can a woman rebut a male rapist's claim that "she asked for it"?

B has a different approach to the role of physical contact in paradigmatic sex. B's view is that feminists should deny that heterosexual procreative sex is the only legitimate or real sex, thereby affirming the existence of lesbian, gay, and bi-sexuality and freeing women's passion from patriarchal definition and control. Further, female autoeroticism is as much "real sex" as is heterosexual intercourse , and the reality of autoerotic sex is not diminished by the agent's conjuring up imaginary lovers. From this perspective, it appears arbitrary to deny the reality of sex in which a virtual lover is summoned via the Internet.

Both A and B make useful points. If a feminist theory of committed relationship is going to prohibit extra-relationship sex, it will need to define what counts as sex. One problem is that once having agreed that sex need not be about procreation, and that a sexual episode should not be identified straightforwardly with the rise and fall of some penis but comprises many forms of touch and interwoven fantasy, it is not obvious that sex need involve flesh at all. However, there is something worrisome about a proposal to define sex as essentially mental and only contingently embodied activity (as in the popular quip, "The biggest sex organ is the brain.") According to many theorists, women are aligned on the deprecated side of a series of post-cartesian dichotomies: mind/matter, soul/body, subject/object, male/female. Hence, in this cultural context, women are liable to be regarded as mindless material objects available to be worked on, given desirable form by, male mental activity. If sex were to be understood as essentially mental activity, this might legitimate the forcible remodeling of women in accordance with male sexual imaginings characteristic of pornography. While it is hard to validate such broad claims, it is notable that much current cyber technology encourages the experience of sexual activity as the manipulation of docile, female bodies by disembodied male minds (c.f. Penthouse's "interactive" CD-ROM, in which the user can "select," "strip," and "pose" female models according to his desires).Further, despite some pundits' endorsement of the new technologies as potentially female- and feminist-friendly, current studies suggest that the Net remains a de facto male-dominated domain.

Let us return to A and B. A might have argued differently in case 1, conceding to B that the on-line affair was indeed sexual, but that sexual fidelity is not central to a committed relationship. Thus A replies: "Yes, I have engaged in meaningless sex with C, but that does not mean I do not love you. What is central to a committed relationship is a special emotional bond with one's partner, and that bond is independent of sex."

This response puts B in a different position. B may believe A's claim that the sex with C meant nothing special to A, confirming that A is capable of meaningless sex. Then B must believe that, on some past occasions, A's sexual engagements with B may have had no special meaning to A, expressing no positive emotional attitude to B. If B believed that sex carries a special expressive meaning, this revelation of A's may cast a disconcerting new light over their shared sexual history.

On the other hand, B may believe that sex does always carry a special meaning for A; thus, when A had cybersex with C, A was expressing love for someone other than B. If B believes that love is by definition exclusive, B will regard A's cybersex adventures as proof that A no longer loves B.

Assuming we have agreed on what counts as sex, we then have to figure out whether to require sexual fidelity of participants in a committed relationship and on what grounds. From a feminist perspective, it is hard to see why extra-relationship sex would be wrong in itself. The traditional prohibition on adultery was always enforced on wives but not husbands, leading to the suspicion that the reason for the prohibition in the marriage model is simply to prevent cuckolded men from unwittingly taking care of other men's sons.

On the other hand, if one retains the romantic account of sex as properly an expression of love, extra-relationship sex may be condemned on the different grounds that it expresses love for someone else outside the relationship. On this view, extra-relationship sex would be derivatively wrong, as a sign of emotional infidelity.

Again, let us assume that A and B are both feminists. Why might B affirm and A deny that sex should be understood and preserved as a special medium for expressing emotional bonds between adults?

B begins: "I can imagine other human societies in which sex carries no special expressive meaning, in which having sex with another is regarded as no more significant than eating together. However, as it happens, in our culture, sexual intimacy has come to be experienced as a profound manner of access to the self. Hence, permitting someone sexual access is regarded as a sign of affection and trust. One cannot erase this meaning casually or by individual fiat. In the context of our culture, in which our senses of who we are have been formed, it is self-deceptive or irresponsible to recommend that sex be undertaken as an activity with no freight of meaning. That sex is experienced as having a special connection to one's sense of self is suggested by responses to unchosen sex. Feminists have documented the trauma of rape as an assault on the inner self and the peculiarly damaging effects of rape within trusting relationships. One cannot easily compare a case in which a father forces his daughter to eat with him and a case of incestuous rape. The point here is not to downgrade other forms of suffering, but to suggest that, given our cultural context, sex does carry a particular value."

A counters that B's view ignores the sexual double standard in patriarchy. "In fact," A argues, "sex and love are strongly associated in women's minds, but not in men's—a discrepancy produced by the ideology of romantic love, which exists to limit women's sexual passion to the production of legitimate male heirs for their husbands. Given this reading of the cultural context, demystification of sex is in order. Just as women need to escape the idea that they can only love men, so they need to be rid of the idea that they can only have or enjoy sex with someone they love, for these are twin aspects of the same ideology. As in all decent human interactions, so too in sex, one must respect the other's wishes. Beyond this, sex is permissible in any consensual adult context, be it sought for pleasure, profit, or procreation."

B replies that A's strategy of demystifying sex will inevitably be subverted under capitalist patriarchy. "Endorsing sex without love just accelerates the alienation from every aspect of one's being characteristic of advanced capitalism, as every human capacity is commodified, drained of meaning, and subjected to the rules of exchange value. Feminists should resist this reductivism, particularly as it is women's bodies that are the primary targets of sexual objectification and exploitation by the captains of the global sex industry. Despite unease at occasionally seeming to share a platform with religious right-wingers, we should preserve the sense that sex is a special mode of human interaction, expressive of the non-fungibility of the beloved particular other, most appropriate, therefore, within a committed relationship."

I'm not sure that I can find strong feminist reasons for requiring committed partners to abstain from extra-relationship sex. Clearly, if extra-relationship sex involves a breach of promise, or deception, then it is wrong, but not on peculiarly feminist grounds. And it is not yet clear whether all feminist committed relationships must, as such, be founded on a promise of exclusive sexual access, or of perfect, mutual self-disclosure.

On the other hand, a form of the romantic idea that sex should be cherished as a special medium for expressing love can be defended, following the line of thought above about the risks of construing sex as primarily a mental activity. The argument would center on the idea that sex offers an unique context for re-integrating one's physical and psychological person. Though I have mostly found this idea articulated by non-fenimist thinkers, some feminist critiques of prostitution rely on a version of this thought However, unless maintaining a committed relationship requires that one forgo all strong emotional ties to other adults, this rewritten romanticism still does not justify a ban on extra-relationship sex.

The Case of Cyber Love

Let us turn now to consider directly the idea that committed relationships are centrally a matter of exclusive emotional attitudes, and consider case 2, the cyber-affair of the heart. In case 2, A stands accused of emotional adultery: A has allowed someone other than

B, A's partner in a committed relationship, a privileged kind of emotional access to A. Again, A may try various lines of defense: arguing that what A is doing on-line is not really emotional adultery, for it is merely fictional ("Cyber-confiding is like having an imaginary friend, it's not really part of my real life the way you are, B"), insincere ("I was only faking my affection for C, I didn't mean it"), or that emotional monogamy is not central to committed relationships ("Loving C does not conflict with my love for and commitment to you, B").

Let us begin by assuming that it is wrong to disclose emotionally to someone other than one's partner in committed relationship. Emotional disclosure either matters in itself, or because it is believed to be a reliable expression of love. The logic of A's self-defense must be rather different in the case of emotional adultery from that of sexual adultery. One can, of course, deceive others about the nature of one's emotional or sexual experience: one can tell lies about one's feelings, just as one can fake orgasm. Sincere and explicit talk about sex may not amount to sex: as we saw above, it takes some argument to establish that talk about sex really is sex, rather than merely flirtation. However, if one's talk is sincere, explicit talk about feelings just is emotional disclosure. So A's claim that intimate emotional disclosure to C is "merely fictional" is less likely to convince than the claim that cybersex is "merely fictional."

To establish a distance between real and fictional emotional disclosure, A re-invokes a distinction between A's "real self" and A*, A's on-line persona. What A types on-line to C is a description of the inner life of A*, the fictional character, which is to be distinguished from A's emotional disclosures to B in real life. Making this distinction allows A to claim that A* is not disclosing insincerely to C, but what A* discloses is not A's inner life, which is shared only with B, hence no emotional adultery has occurred.

B objects that A is accused not just of telling intimate secrets, but also of encouraging another's confidences. So even though A*'s tales may be artful fictions, with no relation to how A really feels, still, A, and not A*, is C's confidante. Since A* is a fictional character, A* is not alive, and something non-living can be neither a sympathetic nor an unsympathetic confidante, any more than a rock can be one. To deny responsibility for emotional adultery on the grounds that you did not speak, but only listened, is as disingenuous as claiming that you are not responsible for sexual adultery on the grounds that you took a passive and not an active role in sex. B remains upset.

A responds that B is blurring once again the bounds of fact and fiction, thought and deed, and that these boundaries are crucial for feminism. Again, a cyber-affair of the heart is no more than a romantic fiction with two authors: for all A knows, C's "intimate disclosures" were no more accurate descriptions of C's author's true feelings than A*'s were of A's. Again, C could be a bot, whose responses to A*'s cues are just expressions of C's program, not a heart overflowing with authentic sentiment. If A's cyber-romance is objectionable, so, too, is B's habit of reading romance novels. B is putty in the hands of the skilled novelist, who is able to anticipate the response of the average romance reader, just as much as A is in thrall to C's programmer's ability to predict and gratify the response of the average net nerd. B's desire to restrain A's gratification by on-line fictions is a covert way of trying to colonize A's imagination.

The idea of "emotional adultery" thus raises two important questions for the project of composing a feminist theory of committed relationship: (1) Is intimate disclosure of one's inner life to someone outside the relationship prohibited by a committed relationship? and (2) Is intimate disclosure of one's inner life to one's partner a necessary condition of committed relationship?

On the first point, there is no reason to think that intimate disclosure of one's inner life to someone outside the relationship should be prohibited by a feminist model of committed relationship. It is, of course, prima facie wrong to betray confidences, especially so when the confidante is an intimate, for one may thereby shatter the basis for her trust in others more generally. However, disclosure of my inner life to someone outside the relationship need not entail the betrayal of any of my partner's secrets, unless my inner life is simply a repository for the other's secrets. Thus, if my partner treats my sharing my feelings with another as equivalent to a betrayal of his or her secrets, my partner must regard my inner life as just such a repository. This is an unacceptable view, for it reduces one's partner's subjectivity to a mirror or storehouse of one's own concerns. Moreover, empirical studies of women's support networks show the practical importance to women's well-being of disclosing relationships with others outside a committed, two-person relationship.

Is intimate disclosure of one's inner life a necessary condition of a committed relationship? One can find feminist prima facie reasons either way. On the one hand, there is a body of evidence that strongly suggests many contemporary women regard sharing their inner lives through intimate talk as a highly desirable part of a committed relationship, although this desire appears to be an historically recent phenomenon, at least in heterosexual relationships. Feminist theorists should pay due attention to the announced desires of actual women. Some female advocates of the merits of on-line relationships point out that they require much greater communicativeness between partners than do body-based affairs: in real life one may stare moodily into one's martini as a seduction strategy; on-line, the strong and silent stranger literally vanishes from the screen.

On the other hand, there are good reasons for feminists to avoid recommending a "therapeutized" model of relationship, in which talking about feelings becomes the main goal of maintaining relationships, thereby dislocating partners from any broader sphere of external political activity. Further, endlessly "processing one's relationship" may distort one's understanding of power in relationships, analyzing problems simply as arising from individual psychological features, when they may depend on structural aspects of external society (e.g., stereotypes about individuals qua members of particular groups).

It is also important for a feminist theory of committed relationship to provide women with a critical perspective on their own desires, for them to reflect on what they truly want and on what is worth wanting. It may be that women misidentify what they want, when they say they want their male partners to be more communicative about their inner feelings. Perhaps some women regard the flux of their male partner's inner life as the source of his subsequent actions, so that the woman's announced desire for access to this inner life is really an unrecognized desire to participate equally in making decisions that affect the partnership, rather than simply to be presented with his decisions. To take another example, perhaps some women who lament their female partners' non-communicativeness about feelings are also expressing a desire for a new vocabulary adequate to articulate lesbian experiences of relationship. Finally, it might be that what matters for committed relationships about intimate disclosure of feelings is that there be an equal division of emotional labor between the partners.

Although the above discussions raise many more issues than I have been able to resolve, let me turn to my provisional, positive recommendations. The form of fidelity in committed relationships most clearly worth feminist advocacy at present is something I call "practical fidelity," rather than sexual or emotional fidelity. To make this case, let me briefly characterize what I take practical fidelity to be and why it is largely lacking in cyber-relationships.

Some people have undertaken relationships entirely in cyberspace, "meeting," "courting," even "marrying" and "breaking up" on-line, and report that they derive important kinds of sexual and emotional satisfaction from these affairs. Some women report that they have had important and empowering experiences in conducting relationships on-line: for example, trying out different gender roles, being perceived as attractive when in real life they are told they are ugly because of standards of physical beauty for females that they do not meet, and so on. I do not dismiss the importance of such relationships: they can provide satisfaction whilst they endure, and also have beneficial effects in enabling people subsequently to behave differently in real life. However, such "disembodied affairs" cannot yield a key good of committed relationship, namely, practical help in one's everyday life.

By this, I have in mind performing simple domestic tasks like sharing the preparation of meals, cleaning, taking care of each other when ill, and taking care of children, if partners have them. These are all activities that are closely related to our embodied nature. Defenders of on-line relationships may reasonably point out that people receive all kinds of practical advice and emotional support from e-mail discussion lists and on-line communities like Stacy Horn's Echo. One might go further and argue that as the technology becomes more sophisticated, cyber friends will be able to help each other in practical ways: when it becomes possible for me to turn on the stove in my own home from my workstation in the office, it will also become possible for me to turn on my friend's for her.

Right now, futuristic speculations on the development of new technologies should not distract us from the present material conditions of actual women's existence. It may be that on-line relationships will ultimately provide (at least some of) us with a new language of committed relationship, an egalitarian lyric poetry of emoticons and gender-ambiguous eroticism. However, we should also recall that right now, women students cannot stay late e-mailing at the college computer lab, for fear of assault on the way home; right now, Hispanic women are working for exploitative wages in Silicon Valley, to ensure that computer executives come in to clean offices every morning.

What has this outburst to do with practical fidelity and feminist committed relationships? Two key challenges for contemporary feminism in the post-industrial West arise in the sphere of personal relationships: one is to end the exploitation of women's domestic labor, and the other is to end domestic violence. Both of these challenges are to do with the disposition of bodies in relation to each other in the private sphere. The ideal of practical fidelity requires each participant in a committed relationship to be devoted bodily to helping the other as much as s/he is able and to enact in the minutiae of everyday life a respectful concern for the other as an equal.

Much of women's traditional domestic labor is directly to do with tending bodies: keeping bodies clean, fed, healthy, clad, comfortable. It has long been a feminist project to get men to do their fair share of this kind of work, and there have been some improvements in the division of domestic labor in male-female households in North America, while the partnership holds together. However, it is still true that more women than men are working the "double shift" of job and family labor. The service industries that have developed to replace the work of women who are now engaged in paid labor outside the home, such as fast-food outlets, dry-cleaners, daycare centres, are staffed by poorly-paid women, often minority women. Moreover, following divorce or separation of a heterosexual couple with children, the woman continues to do most of the work associated with child-care and often falls into poverty because of this.

Hence, part of the idea of practical fidelity emphasizes the fair division of domestic labor, as well as taking responsibility for the broader issues of social justice that arise when the basic tasks of bodily maintenance listed above are "out-sourced" beyond the household. To give a concrete example: it would be a transgression of practical fidelity to refuse to take one's turn cleaning the bathroom, and it would not fix the problem to hire a maid to do the work in one's place when one's turn came. The latter move imports into the relationship the external world's judgement that the labor of one member (who can afford to pay a maid) of the partnership is more valuable than that of the other (who cannot afford to pay a maid). Further, the maid's value is treated as unconnected to the relation between the partners, and this is clearly not so. Working side by side on domestic chores enacts a recognition that each relationship participant's time and energy matters equally.

On the second key issue, feminist theorists might well react to the high rate of physical violence against women by their intimate male partners by recommending, prudentially, that women conduct relationships with men only in cyberspace, thereby reducing the risks to women of physical damage and rape. Even if one proposed the "cyber-affairs only" rule in the spirit of the Lysistrata, as a way to get men to stop behaving badly, it does not offer a positive alternative picture of what a committed relationship could look like. In particular, normative heterosexuality is not explicitly challenged.

Committed relationships must be understood as relationships that normally take place in the medium of space and time between embodied agents, for it is here that domestic violence takes place and must be stopped. Practical fidelity requires partners to be aware of each other's and one's own physical vulnerability, to refrain from damaging each other, and to take care of each other in practical ways. Iris Marion Young has offered us phenomenological descriptions of the effect of patriarchal oppression on women's felt experience of their own bodies. What we need now is a new choreography for embodied agents, whose physical interactions are governed by the ideal of practical fidelity. Agents governed by this ideal would enact mutual respect and care. One may speculate that the private sphere would feel very different to its inhabitants if both men and women were accorded an equal right to control their own bodies, if women were truly free of the threat of male assault, and if compulsory heterosexuality were dismantled.

12

Internet Education in India

In a vast country such as India using information and communication technologies in distance education mode has the potential for cost-effective in-service education of teachers. As access to the Internet is mainly available to those living in metropolitan cities promotion of its use for education has become a cause of concern for it can only exacerbate the digital divide. The Direct Media Service of the World Space has emerged, as a technology that can bridge the digital divide as it is direct-to-home and uses wireless satellite transmission for delivering multimedia data and voice and can be effectively used for in-service education. In this paper experience of a pilot experiment on in-service education of physics teachers using the Direct Media Service of the World Space in combination with different modes of voice delivery such as satellite radio, FM transmission and the Internet have been described. For the experiment a set of lessons on the Newton's laws of motion and the Newton's bucket experiment were developed as multimedia slides and their transition was synchronised with the audio track of the voice of the expert. The experiments on inset were carried out at New Delhi and Bangalore. About seventy secondary school physics teachers took part in the different experiments described in the paper. Using the software LearnLinc a highly interactive e-leaning environment was created. The analysis of the feedback given by the participants has shown that the instructional objectives were successfully achieved. For arranging interaction of the participants with the expert phone-in and the Internet were tried. Till such time access to the Internet becomes more widespread participants may have to use telephone and/or post for interacting with experts. The footprint of the Direct Media Service beam is more than 14 million square kilometres. The success of the experiment has brought out the possibility of making available quality lessons given by experts throughout the country without requiring use of telephone lines for accessing them from the Internet or their dissemination through CD-ROMs.

The Technologies

Some recent developments in information and communication technologies (ICT) have emerged as viable alternatives that can be effectively used in bridging the digital divide and for delivering learning resources at near zero cost to learners across an entire continent. One such technology that has recently emerged on the scene is the satellite radio services. The satellite radio system combines digital audio and digital data transmission (**Direct Media** Service), two of the most powerful technologies of the Information Age, in the direct-to-home (DTH) mode.

The World Space Radio employs satellite technologies of transmission and geographic reach with a footprint of 14 million square kilometres. That is all users within this area can receive digital sound and digital data with a 10 cm wide satellite antenna.

The World Space offers Direct Media Service (DMS), a unique facility of delivering huge amounts of web enabled data to a user's PC by transmission from a satellite. The user's PC is connected to a World Space digital receiver coupled with a PC Adapter or is provided with a PC Receiver Card. Data is loaded directly in the hard drive of the user's Pentium-class PC, without the need for a telephone line or connection to an Internet Service Provider. DMS is a one-way broadcast system and is not an interactive Internet system.

DMS supplements traditional Internet services by offering delivery of gigabytes of popular, educational and informative web-style content without "per-minute" telephone line charges. It is like getting a CD-ROM filled with web content, delivered right to your PC every day. Regarding the speed of delivery of data, the download rate can be as high as 128 kbps. The download occurs automatically and that too unattended, while user may be at work or otherwise engaged. Access to cached content, therefore, seems virtually instantaneous, like a high-speed connection or a CD-ROM.

Combining DMS with terrestrial Radio broadcast opens up yet another possibility for distance education. FM broadcast is an alternative voice delivery mode. It has an advantage over the satellite radio as it can be used for arranging interaction of listeners located within the range of the broadcast station with experts through phone-in facility. Slides to be viewed with audio broadcast may be delivered to users as hardcopies or on CD-ROM or could be accessed from Internet Web Page.

Yet another option for accessing sound files is from the Internet, as compressed sound files of high audio quality can be easily accessed through the Internet using the MP3 technology. As mentioned in the preceding paragraph the slides to be viewed can also be accessed from Internet Web Page. With the synchronisation of audio tracks with slides, which can be easily arranged, multimedia files can be viewed through Web Browser software such as the 'Internet Explorer or as a slide show using the 'Microsoft Power Point' type of software. The audio/text conferencing facility of the Internet has emerged as an effective mode for arranging interaction among a large number of persons sharing common interests.

Another method of delivering multimedia lesson can be through special purpose software product that connects many users to network their systems with that of the teacher through a centralised Internet server system.

Various technology options described briefly in the preceding paragraphs can be used for teaching in synchronous and asynchronous modes with traditional supports like emulated electronic board etc.

The Participating Agencies

The National Council for Teacher Education (**NCTE**) recently carried out experiments on in-service education of physics teachers by using various combinations of the ICT mentioned in the preceding paragraphs. The experiment was a collaborative effort of several organisations. The principal organisations that participated in these experiments were the Indira Gandhi National Open University (IGNOU), UNESCO (made available partial fund support for meeting the transmission costs and for research), World Space Asia (India) and the Satyam Infoway.

In this context it may be of interest to those engaged in distance education to know of the various steps involved in carrying out this experiment. These steps were: the development of the multimedia courseware, use of different delivery modes such as data casting using satellite radio and the Internet, broadcast of sound track by using satellite radio and independently through FM transmission, and feedback of the target group for finding the effectiveness of the various approaches and for its improvement.

The steps involved in the development of the courseware for the experiment were:

voice recording of the lesson delivered by the expert, editing of the sound file, preparation of multimedia Power Point slides using the notes of the expert, checking of the content accuracy of the slides by the expert and synchronisation of the sound file with the slide show. The sound files and the data files were then sent to the World Space transmission hubs at Singapore and Melbourne and were also posted on a Web site for asynchronous downloading and use.

The Lesson

The target group for this experiment was secondary school physics teachers. For this experiment two lessons in physics were used, one was on teaching of the Newton's laws of motion and the other was on the Newton's bucket experiment for explaining concepts of absolute space, inertial and non-inertial frames of reference. Teaching of the Newton's laws of motion is universally found difficult by teachers because students come with their common-sense explanations of physical phenomena and find concepts such as force, acceleration and application of laws of motion difficult to comprehend. The lessons were developed by taking up a set of questions from elementary mechanics and answering them by identifying forces using free-body-diagram, highlighting the correct application of the laws of motion and pointing out the care required in using the third law of motion and the second law of motion.

The lesson was recorded on 3rd November 2001 in the studio of the Educational Media and Production Centre (EMPC), IGNOU, and converted into an audio CD. The audio CD was edited and converted into audio files suitable for broadcast by satellite radio and/or FM, and for download using the Internet. Using the notes of the teacher a storyboard was drawn up for preparing the slides for the lesson. The slides were supported with graphics, animation, text and mathematical equations and were designed and made by Krishna Moorthy, a software expert, who also played the role of coordinator for the experiment, as participation of several agencies was involved. The slide transition was timed for synchronisation with the audio track. In consultation with the content expert of the lesson the data files and the audio files were finalised and delivered to the World Space for data casting and broadcast.

The Experiment

The first experiment was carried out on 27th November 2001 at the EMPC. The data files were delivered to a computer in the EMPC provided with a PC Adapter and connected to a satellite radio antenna. The World Space broadcast the sound at 2 p.m. and the programme was viewed by a select group of audience comprising of educationists, teacher educators, science communicators, heads of schools, physics teachers and the faculty of the IGNOU.

The second experiment was carried out at Bangalore on 28th November at the Regional Centre, IGNOU. About 25 physics teachers from schools in Bangalore attended the lesson. The participants saw the slide show on a screen. A LCD projector was used for the slide show by activating the data file from a computer. The Bangalore Station of the All India Radio on Gyanvani, the FM channel of the IGNOU, broadcast the sound track. After the lesson was over the participant teachers interacted with the expert using the phone-in. The participants were requested to fill-in the tool questionnaire for knowing the usefulness of the approach for in-service education.

The third experiment was carried out on 29th November at the Bangalore Centre of the Satyam Infoway. The 34 physics teachers who took part in this experiment were divided into two groups. One group attended an online virtual class taken by the expert using the software LearnLinc. The other group received the lesson delivered by live demonstration of data casting using the satellite from the up-link hub at Melbourne and broadcast of the sound track from the up-link hub of the World Space at Singapore. All the participant teachers filled the questionnaire and then interacted with the content expert, software expert and the experts of the Satyam Infoway, which is one of the leading Internet service providers.

The Feedback

The feedback of the participants has been analysed. It would suffice to mention that 96% of the participants of the programme held on 28th November (Gyanvani FM transmission) and 100% of the participants of the programme held on 29th November (DMS and interactive virtual classroom) have responded that the objectives of the teaching were attained. Seventy six percent of the participants have suggested that other topics may also be covered using the approach. Sixty seven percent of the participants found sound received at their workstations from the World Space to be of high quality and 23% rated it to be adequate. The quality of sound delivered by FM broadcast was found to be adequate by 52% and 28% rated it to be of poor quality. This was perhaps due to poor signal and can be easily improved by using outdoor antenna. Eighty percent of participants found communication of ideas being discussed in the lesson good and clear. On the whole it can be concluded that the experiment was successful in meeting its objectives.

The success of the experiment (see survey results) in achieving the targeted outcomes have opened the possibility of delivering multimedia learning resources by different techniques to learners directly at their homes, without requiring telephone connections or incurring substantial recurring expenses. The approach used in the pilot experiment has far reaching implications in meeting the goal of providing quality learning resources at an affordable cost by tailor-making them for meeting the varying needs of the entire spectrum of education spanning from school education to professional education.

The Task Ahead

The experience of this pilot experiment on distance education using the World Space system has brought out that it offers itself as a cost-effective technology for delivering quality lessons across the country. The cost of delivery to one user is the same as that of delivering it say to million users. What needs to be done is to identify good teachers from across the country and producing courseware using their expertise. It may not be necessary to bring them to a studio for recording of their lessons. Using cordless microphone recording of their teaching can be done live from their classrooms. By taking pictures of the blackboard work using digital camera and noting time of pictures taken during the progress of the lesson, work of synchronisation of the sound track with the visuals can be carried out without putting inordinate demand on the time of the expert. This approach can be used for distance education of students as well as for in-service education of teachers. For making it viable what is required is sharing of the cost of the transponder by national organisations functioning at different levels of education. The cost of the digital radio receivers will also come down with the increase in its demand. As has already been mentioned, the satellite digital radio offers itself in bridging the digital divide as it is direct-to-home and its bandwidth is adequate for carrying CD quality sound and wireless delivery of data. The challenge is to utilise it by integrating it with other information and communication technologies such as the Internet not only for asynchronous use but more for synchronous interaction of the learners with experts. The courseware can be repackaged on CD-ROM for offline use.

References

1. **Satellite Radio: WorldSpace Radio**

URL: *http://www.worldspace.com*

URL: *www.worldspace.i-p.com*

(World Space supports digital broadcast of audio and multimedia programs directly from satellites to compact, portable receivers. World

Space system is the sole provider of wireless satellite digital audio and multimedia. with potential of providing access to 80 percent of humanity)

2. **Presentation Manager: MS-PowerPoint**

   URL: *http://www.microsoft.com/office/powerpoint/default.htm*

   (It gives easy-to-use tools for creating professional presentations. MS PowerPoint provides slide show supports and automatic conversion of PowerPoint files to Internet compatible html files)

3. **WAVE-to MP3 Converter**

   URL: http: / /*www.mediamatrixes.com/mp3converter/*

   URL: *http://www.futurehits.co.uk/software/mp3encoders.html*

   (Audio encoding software featuring high audio fidelity, multiple file output format, execution of external commands after a file is encoded, flexibility in handling batch processing and more. All programs support conversion of wave files to MP3 files)

4. **LearnLinc: Internet online Classroom**

   URL: *http://www.brandonu.ca/etu/llinc.cfm*

   (LearnLinc is a PC-based learning environment that offers instructor led, live interactive classes to geographically dispersed students. LearnLinc offers different communications options for instructor/ student and student/student communication such as audio graphics and videoconferencing)

Table 1

S. No.	Media source		Delivery modes	
	Audio	Visuals	Audio/Visuals	Interactivity
1	Audio CD	Hard Copy of visuals	Terrestrial radio/ hard copy*	Postal mail/ telephone (offline)
2	Audio CD	Hard copy of visuals	Sattelite radio/hard copy*	Post mail/telphone (offline)
3	Audio CD	Slides (through presentation managers)	Terrestrial radio/ slide show	Telephone/Email Internet (online)
4	Audio CD	Slides through presenttaion managers)	Sattellite radio/DMS	Internet/E-mail

S. No.	Media source		Delivery modes	
	Audio	Visuals	Audio/Visuals	Interactivity
5	Digital CD	Digital CD	Digital CD	Email/Internet (offline)
6	VCD	VCD	VCD	E-mail/Internet (Offline)
7	Beta Tape	Beta Tape	Beta Tape (For TV transmission)*	Telephone/ Internet
8	MP3 Files	Slides (through presentation managers)	Internet (asynchronous)	E-mail
9	Internet Radio	Internet video	Internet (synchronous)	Live

Table 2: Survey Results Attainment of the objectives of the teaching

Response	Gyanvani (Terrestrial Radio)	World Space (Satellite Radio)	LearnLinc (Internet online classroom)
Yes	96%	89%	100%
No	4%	11%	0%

Table 3: Effectiveness of the communication of the ideas

Response	Gyanvani (Terrestrial Radio)	World Space (Satellite Radio)	LearnLinc (Internet online classroom)
Very good	80%	100%	56%
Satisfactory	20%	0%	44%

Table 4: Clarity of the visuals used in the lessons

Response	Gyanvani (Terrestrial Radio)	World Space (Satellite Radio)	LearnLinc (Internet online classroom)
Very good	84%	100%	81%
Satisfactory	12%	0%	19%
Needs improvement	84%	100%	81%

Table 5: Audio/Visual synchronisation

Response	Gyanvani (Terrestrial Radio)	World Space (Satellite Radio)	LearnLinc (Internet online classroom)
Very good	56%	83%	31%
Satisfactory	44%	17%	56%
Needs improvement	0%	0%	13%

Bibliography

Anderson, J. R., A. T. Corbett, K. Koedinger, and R. Pelletier. "Cognitive Tutors: Lessons Learned", *The Journal of the Learning Sciences*, Vol. 4, Issue 2, 1995, pp. 167-207.

Anderson, R. H., T. K. Bikson, S. A. Law, B. Mitchell, C. Kedzie, B. Keltner , C. W. Panis, J. Pliskin, and P. Srinagesh. *Universal Access to E-Mail: Feasibility and Societal Implications*, Santa Monica, Calif.: RAND, MR-650-MF, 1995.

Cuban, L. *Teachers and Machines*, New York: Teachers College Press, 1986.

Dewar, J. *The Information Age and the Printing Press: Looking Backward to See Ahead*, Santa Monica, Calif.: RAND P-8014, 1998.

Dwyer, D. "Apple Classrooms of Tomorrow: What We've Learned", *Educational Leadership*, April 1994, pp. 4-10.

Fletcher, D. The Effectiveness and Cost of Interactive Videodisc Instruction, *Machine-Mediated Learning*, 3, 1989, pp. 361-385.

Gomez, L. M., and D. N. Gordin. Establishing Project-Enhanced Classrooms Through Design, in D. Jonassen and G. McCalla, eds., *Proceedings of the International Conference on Computers in Education*, Charlottesville, Va.: AACE, 1996.

Hall, B.. "Return on Investment and Multimedia Training", *Multimedia Training and Internet Newsletter*, July-August 1995.

Katz, S., A. Lesgold, G. Eggan, and M. Gordin. "Modeling the Student in SHERLOCK II", *Journal of Artificial Intelligence and Education* (Special Issue on Student Modeling), Vol. 3, No. 4, 1993, pp. 495-518.

Kulik, J. A. Meta-analytic Studies of Findings on Computer-Based Instruction, in E. L. Baker and H. F. O'Neil, eds., *Technology Assessment in Education and Training,*. Hillsdale, N.J.: LEA Publishers, 1994.

McArthur, D., and M. Lewis. "Muddy Learning: Evaluating Learning in Multi-User Computer-Based Environments", unpublished, 1996.

McEldowney, P. "Scholarly Electronic Journals — Trends and Academic Attitudes: A Research Proposal"(URL http://poe.acc.virginia.edu/~pm9k/libsci/ejs.html), 1995.

Perraton, H. Comparative Cost of Distance Teaching in Higher Education: Scale and Quality, in G. P. K. Ip Dhanarajan, K. S.M Yuen, and C Swales, eds., *Economics of Distance Learning,* Hong Kong: Open Learning Press, 1994.

Postman, N. *The End of Education: Redefining the Value of School,* New York: Alfred A. Knopf, 1995.

Resnick, M. *Turtles, Termites, and Traffic Jams: Explorations in Massively Parallel Microworlds,* Cambridge, Mass.: MIT Press, 1994.

Rosen, S. "The Economics of Superstars", *American Economic Review,* Vol. 71, No. 5, 1981, pp. 845-858.

Rothenberg, J. "Ensuring the Longevity of Digital Documents", *Scientific American,* January 1995, pp. 24-29.

Stoll, C. *Silicon Snake Oil: Second Thoughts on the Information Highway,* New York: Doubleday Anchor Books, 1995.

Tyack, L., and L. Cuban. *Tinkering Toward Utopia,* Cambridge, Mass.: Harvard University Press, 1995.

INDEX